ON ALEXANDER'S TRACK TO THE INDUS

ON ALEXANDER'S TRACK TO THE INDUS:

PERSONAL NARRATIVE OF EXPLORATIONS ON THE NORTH-WEST FRONTIER OF INDIA

AUREL STEIN

GYAN

Published by

GYAN

Gyan Publishing House
5, Ansari Road
Daryaganj, New Delhi-110002
Phone: 011-47034999, 9811692060
E-mail: books@gyanbooks.com

Distribution Network
gyanbooks.com
India, USA, Canada, UK, Australia

ISBN: 978-93-7133-117-3 (HB)

First Published, 1899

2nd Impression 2025

Printed at: Gyan Press, Delhi.

ON ALEXANDER'S TRACK TO THE INDUS: PERSONAL NARRATIVE OF EXPLORATIONS ON THE NORTH-WEST FRONTIER OF INDIA
Author: AUREL STEIN

ON ALEXANDER'S TRACK
TO THE INDUS

RUINED BUDDHIST STŪPA OF TŌP-DARA, ABOVE HAIBAT-GRĀM.

ON ALEXANDER'S TRACK TO THE INDUS

PERSONAL NARRATIVE OF EXPLORATIONS ON THE NORTH-WEST FRONTIER OF INDIA

CARRIED OUT UNDER THE ORDERS OF H.M. INDIAN GOVERNMENT BY

SIR AUREL STEIN, K.C.I.E.
INDIAN ARCHAEOLOGICAL SURVEY

1929

TO THE MEMORY OF

COLONEL SIR HAROLD DEANE, K.C.S.I.

THE GREAT WARDEN OF THE

INDIAN NORTH-WEST MARCHES

THIS RECORD IS INSCRIBED

IN GRATEFUL REMEMBRANCE

AND SINCERE ADMIRATION

PREFACE

THE explorations described in these pages had for their scene a region beyond the administrative border of the Indian North-West Frontier not previously accessible to Europeans. In the initial chapter of this volume a brief account will be found of those recent developments in 'tribal politics' which through the rise to power of a strong and capable ruler in the person of the Miāngul Bādshāh, now 'Wālī of Swāt', brought peace to a land singularly favoured by nature but for centuries torn by the discord of man. For the enlightened spirit with which he welcomed my visit and for the unfailing help and care by which he rendered my travels both safe and fruitful, I shall ever cherish deep gratitude. But equally grateful I feel to those kind friends on this side of the border whose willingly offered support, as recorded in the same chapter, made it possible for me to explore that fascinating country under the generous auspices of H.M.'s Indian Government.

A kindly Fate, and sympathetic comprehension on the part of those who officially dispense it, have enabled me, during intervals of my forty-one years' Indian service, to carry out explorations over the greater part of Innermost Asia, and along the whole of those north-western borderlands of India which by their historical past have powerfully attracted me since my early youth. These travels, devoted to antiquarian and geographical research, have taken me from westernmost China right through Central Asia and from the snowy Pāmīr ranges down to the desolate coast of the Ikhthyophagoi by the Arabian Sea. But nowhere did they touch ground so replete with historical interest as in that comparatively small area to the west of the Indus which Alexander's march of conquest towards India for a brief span of time illuminates as it were with the light of a meteor.

It was the main object of my tour to follow up the track of the great Macedonian in this region so far as it is at present accessible outside Afghānistān. The classical records of his campaign would alone suffice to invest these parts with a special human interest. But their history has been so exceptionally varied and eventful at other periods also, that a rapid review of it seems here justified, be it only to provide the right background for what the country reveals to us in the life of its present day and in the silent ruins of its past.

We have grown accustomed to divide the ancient world, as some do the modern, between East and West. But in many ways India stands apart, separated from either by its own ancient civilization, just as it is fenced off geographically by the ocean and great mountain ramparts. It is on this part of the North-West Frontier, where the main routes of trade and migration debouch from the Afghān highlands, that India, before modern times, came chiefly into contact both with the East and the West.

Long before Alexander's invasion produced the first direct impact of the West on India, the great valleys of Peshawar and Swāt had seen the descent of conquerors from that part of the true East which we know as Īrān. The victory won in prehistoric times by an invading Aryan chief on the banks of the Suvāstu, the Swāt river, is sung already in a hymn of the Rigveda. Gandhāra, comprising the present Peshawar district with the neighbouring tracts, figures among the provinces that the great Darius had secured for the Persian empire of the Achaemenidian kings of kings.

Alexander's triumphant invasion passed by, indeed, without leaving a trace in Indian literature or tradition. But Hellenistic princes from Bactria, which Alexander had colonized with Greeks, afterwards ruled on both sides of the Indus during a couple of centuries and there kept the door open for influences derived from the classical West. It is a fascinating chapter in history, though we can study it only in the fine Greek-modelled coins of these rulers and in those sculptures of Graeco-Buddhist art which the ruined Buddhist shrines of the Swāt and Peshawar valleys have preserved for us.

Then when the great Indo-Scythian empire of the Kushān dynasty had replaced the small Hellenistic chiefships on both sides of the Hindukush and had further extended its sway beyond the Indus, it was from this north-western borderland that fervent religious propaganda carried the Buddha's doctrine, together with Graeco-Buddhist art and Indian literary culture, into Central Asia and thence into China. This spread of Buddhism right across Asia may well be considered India's greatest contribution to the civilization of mankind in general. These fair border valleys, dotted with sacred Buddhist sites, thus acquired special sanctity for monastic communities so far away as the Yellow Sea, and attracted the visits of those pious Chinese pilgrims whose records now serve to guide us among the ruined sanctuaries of Swāt, their *Udyāna*, 'the Garden'.

Without these records we should have scarcely anything to lift the darkness that descended on this region during the centuries when White Hun and Turkish domination succeeded the decay of the Indo-Scythian empire. Declining Buddhism gave way to lingering Hindu worship and this in turn succumbed about A.D. 1000 to the victorious onslaught of Islām under the great Maḥmūd of Ghazna. From the civilization and art which the Muhammadan conquerors of India brought with them out of Īrān, itself fertilized long before by Hellenistic influences, the border tracts could receive but little benefit. They soon became a mere passage land tenanted by warlike Pathān tribes from the hills, ever ready to dispute the 'Gates of India' to any but the strongest of the new foreign rulers of Northern India. The once flourishing territory in which they had settled lapsed more and more into barbarism. The Memoirs of the Emperor Bābar, the great founder of the Moghul Empire in India, have little else to tell of Peshawar and Swāt than tales of frequent hard fighting with the tribes.

The advent of Sikh power, under Mahārāja Ranjit Singh, in the first half of the last century, was but a short-lived reaction from the Indian side; across the Indus its hold was never more than very precarious. Such as it was, the Sikhs were unable to extend it to the Swāt valley, where the tribes under the spiritual leadership of the famous Ākhund of Swāt, the present ruler's grandfather, maintained an uninterrupted independence.

It was left to the British 'Rāj', after the annexation of the Panjāb, to restore peace and steadily reviving prosperity to these border tracts, ravaged by centuries of invasion and internal disorder; and it has been the destiny of British arms to keep watch and ward here ever since. The help I invariably received, wherever my work took me, from the officers who share in the hard task of guarding the Frontier, will, like the friendships I was privileged to form among them, ever rank with the most cherished recollections of my life. It was my good fortune to find the earliest of these ever helpful friends in Colonel Sir Harold Deane, that lamented great Warden of the Marches, who in due course became the first Chief Commissioner of the North-West Frontier Province, and to his memory this volume must be inscribed.

It only remains to record my thanks for help received in connexion with the present publication. They are due to the Government of India for their kind permission to make this account of my tour in Swāt accessible to a wider public and to illustrate it by a selection from the photographs

I took in the course of it. To the Survey of India Department I am indebted for the use of the topographical materials secured with the aid of Surveyor Tōrabāz Khān, who had been deputed by it to accompany me on the journey. The Royal Geographical Society has kindly allowed reproduction of the sketch-map prepared from the original surveys and first published in its *Journal*, while the more detailed map of the Pīr-sar area, where I believe I have located Alexander's Aornos, was drawn and printed under the friendly care of Colonel H. T. Morshead at the Geodetic Survey Office, Dehra Dun. Here I may conveniently also note that the translation of passages in Arrian's *Anabasis* relating to Alexander's campaign between the Panjkōra and Indus has been taken from Mr. McCrindle's *Invasion of India*, with such modifications as examination of the Greek text appeared to me to render desirable.

Finally, I must offer my special thanks to the publishers, who readily agreed to whatever could make this small volume attractive to the eye, and to the Oxford University Press, whose care has greatly facilitated its being satisfactorily passed into print in spite of the great distance at present between us. On a separate page I have thought it useful to name certain publications in which I have recorded observations on the early history and antiquities of the North-West Frontier gathered in the course of former explorations.

AUREL STEIN.

CAMP, MOHAND MARG, KASHMĪR.
September 24, 1928.

Detailed Report on an Archaeological Tour with the Buner Field Force. Lahore, Punjab Government Press, 1898. [Reprinted in the *Indian Antiquary*, Bombay, January–March, 1899.]

Report of Archaeological Survey Work in the North-West Frontier Province and Baluchistan, 1904–5. Peshawar, Government Press, N.W. Frontier Province, 1905.

Ruins of Desert Cathay. Personal Narrative of Explorations in Central Asia and Westernmost China. Volumes I–II. London, Macmillan & Co., 1912.

Annual Report of the Archaeological Survey of India, Frontier Circle, 1911–12. Peshawar, Government Press, N.W. Frontier Province, 1912.

Serindia. Detailed Report of Explorations in Central Asia and Westernmost China. Volumes I–V. Oxford, Clarendon Press, 1921.

'Alexander's Campaign on the Indian North-West Frontier.' London, *Geographical Journal*, November–December, 1927.

Innermost Asia. Detailed Report of Explorations in Central Asia, Kan-su and Eastern Īrān, Volumes I–IV. Oxford, Clarendon Press, 1928.

An Archaeological Tour in Wazīristān and Northern Balūchistān. 'Memoirs' of the Archaeological Survey of India. Calcutta, Government of India Press. [In the press.]

CONTENTS

LIST OF ILLUSTRATIONS

MAPS

CHAPTER I

AN OLD TRANSBORDER GOAL

I SHALL not soon forget the joyful excitement with which, early in December 1925 on arriving at Delhi after a long and busy stay in England, I found awaiting me a letter from Sir Norman Bolton, an old Frontier friend and at that time Chief Commissioner of the North-West Frontier Province, telling me that a goal which I had for many years desired was now at last within my reach. This was the great transborder tract of Upper Swāt and the adjacent valleys, which, by their historic past and the many reported vestiges thereof, had attracted me ever since as a young student, thirty-eight years before, I first came to work on India's ancient soil.

At that time the turbulent independence of Pathān tribes barred the way across the picturesque boldly serrated range that divides the great valley drained by the Swāt river from the open plain of the Peshawar district. The Chitrāl campaign of 1895 had, indeed, opened a route cutting through the lower end of the main Swāt valley, and in the narrow strip of tribal territory thus brought under 'political' control, the friendly interest of Colonel Sir Harold Deane, that lamented Warden of the Marches, had allowed me, in the course of rapid tours both before and after the great Frontier rising of 1897, to examine ruins of Buddhist times. After the latter fanatical upheaval I had had an opportunity of seeing parts of Bunēr, the southernmost tract of this region, while accompanying General Sir Bindon Blood's Field Force on the short punitive expedition of 1898. But when the fighting was ended, the fascinating ground beyond the administrative British border became as much closed as ever to European exploration.

What drew my eyes so eagerly towards Swāt was not

merely the fame that this region, the ancient Uḍḍiyana, had enjoyed in Buddhist tradition, nor the traces that early worship and culture were known to have left there in numerous as yet unsurveyed ruins. Nor was it only the wish to find myself again on the tracks of those old Buddhist pilgrims who travelled from China to the sacred sites of Swāt, and whose footsteps I have had the good fortune to follow in the course of my expeditions through the desert wastes of Innermost Asia and across the high ranges of the Pāmīrs and Hindukush. May the sacred spirit of old Hsüan-tsang, the most famous of those pilgrims and my adopted 'Chinese patron saint', forgive the confession: what attracted me to Swāt far more than such pious memories was the wish to trace the scenes of that arduous campaign of Alexander which brought the great conqueror from the foot of the snowy Hindukush to the Indus, on his way to the triumphant invasion of the Panjāb.

In the autumn of 1904 arrangements made with the neighbouring tribes by Sir Harold Deane, then my chief, had made it possible for me to visit Mount Mahāban, where the south-eastern portion of Bunēr approaches the Indus, ground not previously reached by any European. There I could survey the height on which, by a conjecture widely accepted for half a century, it had been proposed to locate the rock stronghold of Aornos, the scene of the most famous exploit of that campaign. But a careful examination of the topographical features had shown that they could not be reconciled with essential details recorded in the Greek accounts of that celebrated siege. It was a purely negative result, and the state of 'tribal politics' at the time and for nearly two decades afterwards precluded any attempt to search for the true site of Aornos higher up near the right bank of the Indus, in an area to which various considerations then pointed.

It was not until after my return from my third Central-Asian expedition (1913–16), and after calm on the North-West Frontier had followed the stress of the war and the subsequent Afghān aggression, that I was able to resume my attempts to reach this goal. In December 1921 I made a rapid tour along the border of the Hazāra District where it approaches the left bank of the Indus, and tried to gather information bearing on a suggestion first made to me by my lamented friend Colonel R. A. Wauhope, R.E. Thirty years before, on one of the hard-fought Frontier campaigns of which the Black Mountains have been the scene, he had sighted from afar a high spur descending from the Swāt watershed to the right bank of the Indus, and there he thought that a likely location of Aornos, the 'Rock' Alexander had captured, might possibly be looked for. But it was only by actual exploration on the spot that the suggestion could be tested, and my hope of securing a chance for this was frustrated for several years by the political situation, more than usually disturbed, which had then arisen in that transborder region.

The great fertile valley of Swāt, now occupied by Pathān clans from the point where the great glacier-fed river breaks through the alpine gorges of Tōrwāl, can rarely have been long free from internecine feuds since the time, about the fifteenth century, when its present masters conquered it from the original inhabitants of Dard stock. But early in the last century a great Muhammadan saint, the famous Ākhund of Swāt, arose in the land. The spiritual authority exercised by him, until he passed away at a great age, was strong enough to moderate the usual fighting between the rival clans and to unite them whenever aggression threatened, whether from those ruling the plains of Peshawar or from the chiefs who for the time being were masters of the adjacent territories to the east or west. But since the great

Ākhund's death in the seventies, aggravated dissension between the several tribal sections of Upper Swāt had steadily weakened whatever authority was exercised by the Miānguls, the descendants of the saint, and the inheritors, as guardians of his tomb, of a kind of spiritual supremacy.

The opportunity offered by this internal division was seized by neighbouring hill chiefs to gain control over the rich lands of Swāt. The ambitious ruler of Dīr, who held the valleys between Swāt and Chitrāl, was gradually over-running the fertile tracts on the right bank of the river. The Nawāb of Amb and Darband, independent chief on the right bank of the Indus, was invading Bunēr and threatening to absorb the main valley of Swāt from the south-east. By a lucky chance my visit to Darband on the previously mentioned tour of 1921 had allowed me to become acquainted with the Nawāb's son-in-law 'Abdul Jabbār Khān, the descendant of a once influential family driven out of Swāt, just as he was setting out to lead the van of the inroad into Bunēr. A previous attempt of this adventurous young man to establish himself as the Nawāb's cat's-paw in the uppermost tract of Swāt had, indeed, ended in failure. But it had made him acquainted with that mountain spur higher up on the right bank of the Indus in which I was interested, and the information he was thus able to give me proved useful enough in the end.

But fortunately for the modern destinies of Swāt, and incidentally for my own plans of antiquarian exploration, the few years following that chance meeting saw the rise to power in Swāt of a very capable ruler in the person of Miāngul Gul-shāhzāda, the elder of the two surviving grandsons of the great Ākhund. He managed to attach firmly to himself some of the more dependable heads of clans and to organize a kind of feudal force, provided with adequate transport for food-supplies and thus capable of prolonged operations, an unusual thing in Pathān tribal warfare. Thus, after hard struggles, in the course of which his younger brother was killed, he ultimately succeeded in driving out both invaders.

Having thus become undisputed master of Upper Swāt he was soon able to extend his sway to Bunēr, always closely linked by tribal relations with Swāt, and also to the valleys that descend beyond the watershed range towards the Indus. It was not long before the Miāngul, now sole heir to the name, became known to the people by the simple designation of *Bādshāh* or 'ruler'. The new kingdom that his energy and sagacity had built up was soon extended to its proper geographical limits by the annexation of Tōrwāl, the alpine portion of the Swāt valley in which the original Dard population of the country, though converted to Islām, had maintained its independence and distinct language.

The peaceful consolidation of what had been won by the Bādshāh's successes had since been greatly facilitated by the close and friendly relations that he wisely fostered with the administration of the North-West Frontier Province. But even this fortunate concatenation of events might not have sufficed to enable me to realize my long-cherished plan of exploration, had not a kindly Fate during those years placed the Government's diplomatic relations with the new ruler of Swāt in charge of my old and ever helpful friend Colonel E. H. S. James, then Political Agent for Dīr, Swāt, and Chitrāl.

In the summer of 1925 I had written from England to Sir Norman Bolton, Chief Commissioner of the North-West Frontier Province, submitting my proposal. Acting under the instructions kindly given by him, Colonel James succeeded, largely through his personal influence with the ruler, in obtaining his consent to my visit to his territory and to my intended explorations. That I was to be allowed to extend them over the whole of his country instead of the comparatively small area to which my original proposal had applied made me feel still more grateful for the enlightened spirit in which my request had been met by the Bādshāh.

Once assured of his generous welcome, I felt confident that all necessary assistance would likewise be available from the British side, and it was soon forthcoming with a promptness that earned my warm gratitude. The Government of India, on the recommendation of Sir John Marshall, Director-General of Archaeology, readily sanctioned my employment on the proposed tour, together with a grant of Rs. 2,000 to meet incidental expenses. Colonel W. J. Keen, another valued old friend just then officiating at the head of the North-West Frontier administration, greatly encouraged me by his kind personal interest in the enterprise. The Survey of India, which had so often helped to make my travels geographically fruitful, readily agreed to facilitate the survey of a region that was for the most part practically unmapped or very imperfectly known from native route reports, by lending the services of one of its trained Indian Surveyors, together with all necessary instruments.

All this contributed to keep my spirits buoyant during the few months which had to be allowed to pass before the actual start. I knew well that climatic conditions would, until towards the close of winter, greatly hamper or altogether prevent operations on the comparatively high ground to which our explorations were to be extended. On the other hand, I could not altogether keep my thoughts from the risk involved in delay. For who that knows something of 'tribal politics' on the Frontier, could ever feel quite assured that conditions would remain quiet for some months ahead in that volcanic belt beyond the border? How often has it seen the abrupt rise and fall of chiefships, like waves suddenly thrown up by a submarine convulsion!

Fortunately, to Colonel Keen's experienced eye, the 'political barometer' on that side of the Frontier stood at 'fair' for the time being, and his encouraging report lessened the strain of waiting. Moreover, there was plenty of work to keep me occupied during those few months at the capital of New Delhi. Patiently I had to wade through hundreds and hundreds of large proof pages of *Innermost Asia*, the detailed account of my third Central-Asian expedition, and with equal patience to watch the steady progress made in the setting up, photographic reproduction, &c., of all the mural paintings that I had succeeded in bringing away from ruined Buddhist shrines in distant Turkestān.

But great was the relief when by the middle of February I was free to shake the dust of the new Indian capital off my feet—and of its overabundant office files off my mind—in order to gain Kashmīr, the familiar base of all my archaeological enterprises. It was cheering to find myself once again at Srīnagar, even though the great valley had shed all its verdure for wintry bareness, and though those old friends, the great surrounding snow-covered mountains, were hidden by low clouds and mists during most of my stay. After a year and a half spent in 'civilization', whether Western or its Indian imitation, many practical preparations were needed to get my camp ready for field work. But the kindness of my old friend Dr. Ernest Neve, the distinguished head of that great institution, the Church Missionary Society's Hospital, had provided warm and spacious quarters, and I had the ready assistance of old retainers. So after a fortnight's toil, in which office *paperasses* still had a large share, I set out on March 4th for the Frontier.

A day's motor drive of nearly two hundred miles by the Jhelam Valley Road down to Rawalpindi brought welcome rest and warmth. There, at the great military centre of the Panjāb, I was met by Tōrabāz Khān, the hardy Surveyor whom Colonel R. H. Phillimore, Director of the Frontier Circle of the Survey of India, had kindly helped to select for topographical work on my journey. There, too, I was able to secure the loan of the modest armament, four army revolvers, which had suggested itself as a desirable complement to our outfit, in view of the tribal *milieu* I was about to enter. The necessary indent order duly applied for at Delhi had, through some red-tape misadventure, failed to reach the Rawalpindi Arsenal in time. But fortunately a kind friend, Major M. A. L. Gompertz, then on the staff of the Northern Command, was prepared to act as *deus ex machina*, and the issue was duly obtained. So the eyes of my orderly, Shehra Khān, a demobilized veteran from the Salt Range, glistened with pride as he moved off with us to the station in charge of the precious 'small arms and ammunition' to take the train for Peshawar.

CHAPTER II

THE START FOR SWĀT

THEY were a delightful three days that I was able to spend at the Frontier capital after my arrival from Kashmīr. Haunts familiar from the years that I had been stationed there looked doubly attractive in the glorious sunshine that followed the pouring rain in which I had travelled from Rawalpindi. Nor could I have wished to see the bare but beautiful hills that surround the great valley from more pleasant quarters than those which I enjoyed, thanks to Colonel Keen's hospitable welcome to Government House (Fig. 2). They were busy days, too; for in succession came Afrāz-gul Khān, my old travel companion; next Corporal 'Abdul Ghafūr, my new 'handy man' lent from the 1st King George's Own Sappers and Miners; and lastly Tōrabāz Khān, the Afrīdī Surveyor. There was plenty to discuss and arrange at this little mobilization. It was hard for Afrāz-gul, who as a youngster had won his spurs on my third Central-Asian expedition, to renounce his eager wish to join me once more. But he was already under orders to start with Major K. Mason on his Karakoram explorations and could now help only in so far as his own brave example and its rewards would *encourager les autres*.

Nor was it easy to find time for the discussion of all the points connected with my projected tour, first with Colonel Keen, and then also with Mr. H. A. F. Metcalfe, the Political Agent for Swāt, Dīr, and Chitrāl, who was directly concerned with the preparatory arrangements. Mr. Metcalfe had opportunely come down from his post on the Malakand partly for 'political' business and partly, I venture to think, to let Mrs. Metcalfe benefit by the little distractions of the 'Peshawar week' just then in progress. After a recent year of exile at the Kābul Legation they had both thoroughly earned the change. To add to the pleasant impressions of my short stay, there arrived for one night Sir Francis Humphrys, H.B.M.'s Minister at Kābul, and Lady Humphrys, both friends of old Frontier times, on their way through to the Viceroy at Delhi.

So it was almost like a rest when, after all my impedimenta had been dispatched and carpets for distant friends in England bought and packed, I myself, on the morning of March 9th, was whirled off in Mr. Metcalfe's comfortable car for the Malakand. Right through the width of the big Yusufzai plain it took me past Nowshera, now a big Cantonment, and pretty tree-girt Mardān. Those picturesque hills of classical form and bareness, rising like rocky islands above the plain, greeted me once again as they had in April 1906, when I was starting on my second expedition to Chinese Turkestān. How I wished that I had more time to feast my eyes upon them and the verdant expanse of fertile land below! Two hours had sufficed to bring us to Dargai, where the railway, now developed to full broad gauge, aptly ends within the walls and wire entanglements of a prim and somewhat bleak fort.

Then up to the pass the car rushed by that serpentine road which I well remembered seeing in the year that it was built, immediately after the Malakand had been fought for and taken in 1895. But there was a notable change in the landscape. In the valley below, once so barren, a new river leapt and foamed: the Upper Swāt Canal, which, brought through the range by a tunnel over two miles long, now carries fertility to the eastern half of the Yusufzai plain, an emblem of the Pax Britannica. Now that I saw this wonderful canal for the first time 'in being', I did not wonder that its fame had reached so far away as the foot of the T'ien-shan, where in 1908 I had heard honest Turkī cultivators inquiring about it with incredulity.

1. VIEW FROM POLITICAL AGENT'S HOUSE, MALAKAND FORT, TOWARDS LOWER SWĀT VALLEY.

The Pax Britannica had left fresh marks, too, on the once blood-soaked heights of the Malakand (Fig. 1). New bungalows had been built on the steep slopes and the growth of firs and cedars had greatly increased within the area protected by 'tribal-proof' towers and forts. The Political Agent's new house, close to the crest of the spur immediately overlooking the pass, seemed full of the comforts of an up-to-date English home; and Mrs. Metcalfe's care had made it delightfully bright with carpets and flowers—and two splendid specimens of the British Baby. A great change it seemed from the days when I had stayed here with Sir Harold Deane in the winter following the great Swāt uprising, and later when Lady Deane was as yet the only—and wholly unauthorized—lady on the Malakand. What with final preparations, repairs successfully accomplished to a camera which had shared my bad fall at a wire entanglement, and a mail from Europe to attend to, the time I was able to pass in that delightfully hospitable home seemed far too short, though half a night was added to the working day. But the glorious view across the verdant Swāt valley and towards the distant snow peaks to the north-east will ever remain fresh in my memory.

On the morning of the 10th, exactly according to my programme, the start was made. Mr. Metcalfe had been invited by the Miāngul to his 'capital' at Saidu for a day's shoot. So it was the chief's motor-car that carried us down into the valley and then on to Thāna, the biggest village within that strip of Swāt which since the Chitrāl campaign is 'protected territory', with its tribal population controlled by the Political Agent. The fine military road down to the bridge crossing the Swāt river had quickly followed the occupation of 1895, and Chakdara fort, which we passed by the river some three miles before reaching Thāna, had served more than once as my night quarters on my short visits to the ruins of Lower Swāt fully thirty years before. But the change since then in general conditions was very manifest. No doubt the men we met on the road, now shaded by fine trees, were still going about armed as they used to. But no escort of 'Swāt Levies' is now needed here to protect 'Sāhibs', and when the car dropped me at Thāna I could freely choose my camp in the open some little distance from the village. The local Khāns, it is true, took care to have it properly guarded at night-time.

The unmetalled road which continues some twenty miles farther to the Miāngul's 'capital' at Saidu was the latest achievement of the ruler whose protection was now to give me access to a region that had hitherto been wholly closed to Europeans. Mr. Metcalfe met me again on his way down forty-eight hours later, pleased with his bag and fully satisfied as to the Miāngul's friendly disposition towards me. Indeed, nothing could exceed that very capable 'Political's' thoughtful care and kindly interest in my tour.

It was a real joy to find myself in the peace and freedom of my little tent, the true home that I had last enjoyed on a favourite high alp of Kashmīr fully two and a half years before. Pleasant, too, was the feeling that now at last, if all went as I wished and hoped, there would be no need for that incessant 'rush' and anxious calculation of time which had seemed inseparable in the past from all my expeditions great and small. But that strenuous work was not lacking from the start, an account of the next few days would suffice to show, if there were room here to give it in detail. I had decided to stop at Thāna for two nights in order to visit certain ruined sites that I had heard of in the valley and hills to the south, and the day following my arrival served to show how much hard tramping and climbing were necessary if justice was to be done to the interesting remains of Buddhist times which abound in this part of Swāt.

Fertile as Swāt still is, and thickly populated as it once was, the whole of the great valley must have been crowded with Buddhist sanctuaries and religious establishments in the centuries immediately before and after Christ. This explains the care taken by the old Chinese pilgrims to visit Swāt on their way from the Hindukush to the sacred sites of India, and the glowing account that they have left us of the land. No doubt, they and other pious visitors knew also how to appreciate the material attractions of Swāt, the abundance and variety of its produce, its temperate climate, and the beauty of its scenery.

These attractions are significantly reflected in the popular etymology that has transformed the ancient name of the country, *Uḍḍiyana,* into Sanskrit *Udyāna,* the 'Garden', as it meets us in the narrative of old Hsüan-tsang, the most famous of those old Chinese travellers. I have had occasion to discuss their accounts of Swāt in the initial chapter of my *Serindia,* and this is not the place to review them in detail. But since we owe to their records almost all that we know of Swāt during the thousand years or more preceding the Muhammadan conquest, and as the memory of them was constantly with me on my wanderings, I may as well introduce their venerable persons here at the outset.

The earliest of those devoted pilgrims of whom we know was Fa-hsien. After crossing amid many hardships the deserts of the Tārīm basin and the 'Snow Mountains' of the Pāmīrs, he descended from the Hindukush range to Wu-ch'ang or Swāt about A.D. 403. He had made his way down from Darēl through those formidable gorges of the Indus which no European has so far been able to enter, 'over a difficult, precipitous and dangerous road', so his narrative tells us, where rock walls forming the sides of mountains that rise ten thousand feet above the river had to be passed over ladders, 'seven hundred in all'. In Swāt he found 'the religion of Buddha extremely flourishing'. There were altogether five hundred monasteries or Saṅghārāmas where 'wandering mendicant priests were found in everything for three days, after which they were told to shift for themselves'. To two of the few sacred spots in Swāt that Fa-hsien specially mentions, my itinerary will presently take us.

Sung Yün, the next pilgrim whose record has survived, in A.D. 519 also crossed the Pāmīrs to the Oxus. But his party wisely avoided the dreaded route by the Indus, 'where iron chains served for bridges and suspended across the void formed a passage', and reached Swāt by the way of Kāfiristān. Having spent a whole winter and spring in Swāt, Sung Yün has left us a full and enthusiastic description of the country. He found Buddhism still very flourishing there, and the king strictly conforming his conduct to the rules of the Buddha's Law. He describes the climate as temperate, the soil as fertile, and the people as enjoying an abundance of produce. During the night the sound of the temple bells filled the whole country. There was a profusion of fine flowers, which continued in bloom during winter as well as summer. My recollections of the narcissus and other early flowers that I had enjoyed on my former midwinter visits to Lower Swāt, and the loveliness of early spring that soon revealed itself to me higher up the valley, enabled me to appreciate the truth of this reference.

Sung Yün mentions quite a number of spots rendered sacred by legends of the Buddha's presence, both in Swāt proper and Bunēr. But owing to a certain confusion in the sequence of his narrative it might have been difficult to locate them correctly did we not possess the account which Hsüan-tsang, the greatest of pious Chinese travellers, has left us in his *Records of the Western Regions*.

When the famous pilgrim arrived about A.D. 630 from the side of Kābul he found Buddhism fallen low from its once

2. GOVERNMENT HOUSE, PESHAWAR.
Residence of the Chief Commissioner, North-West Frontier Province.

3. RUINED DWELLINGS AND TOWER ON BANDAKAI RIDGE, ABOVE KŌTAH.

flourishing condition. In Swāt, as in the Peshawar valley, the ancient Gandhāra, the White Hun conquest about a century earlier had left sad traces of ruin. Hsüan-tsang describes quite correctly the varied configuration of Swāt, its favourable climate, and the abundance of forest, flowers, and fruit-trees. Its people, he tells us, were of a soft and pusillanimous character, inclined by nature to deceit, and practised in magic crafts. Buddhism was still the predominant form of worship; but of the fourteen hundred monasteries that were said to have once existed by the banks of the *Su-p'o-su-tu* or Swāt river, most were in ruins, and the number of the brethren whom they contained, once reckoned at 18,000, was greatly diminished. Of the monks he significantly records that they were 'fond of reading their texts but were incapable of penetrating their meaning, cultivating instead the science of magical formulas'. I had previously followed the footsteps of my 'Chinese patron saint' through the whole width of Central Asia and a great part of Northern India, and had then learnt to rely on the general accuracy of his topographical indications. In Swāt, too, as well as in Bunēr, we might therefore hope to find in him our safest guide to the sites once sacred to Buddhist worship.

The last of the Chinese visitors we know of was Wu-k'ung. This humble successor to Hsüan-tsang reached Swāt in the year 752 in the suite of a mission which the imperial court had dispatched to the Turkish ruler of the Kābul valley, who then also held Peshawar and Swāt. It was the very time when China's predominance in Central Asia was about to be rudely shaken by Arabs and Tibetans. Wu-k'ung, detained by illness in Gandhāra, subsequently became a Buddhist monk, and after pilgrimages, extending from Kashmīr to the sacred spots of Bihār, settled down in a monastery of the chief place of Swāt.

During his long residence in the country he is said to

have 'visited all the holy vestiges'. But his laconic record has little more to tell us than that he found 'not the slightest difference between what he saw and that which Hsüan-tsang's narrative says'. Wu-k'ung's modest brevity is all the more regrettable because his return journey from Swāt to China would have furnished a story of rare interest; it was accomplished under many difficulties and dangers during the years 783–90, when the very last strongholds of China's Central-Asian power succumbed to the attacks of Turks and Tibetans.

CHAPTER III

VISITS TO BUDDHIST RUINS

FROM the scanty records of these pilgrims, distant in time and race, I may now turn to the first days spent among the silent ruins that alone remain of the Buddhist Swāt of their age. A long excursion on March 11th took me up the wide valley to the south through which lead the approaches to the passes of Charāt and Mōra. Both passes cross the watershed towards the Yusufzai plain and are marked by remains of ancient bridle-roads, no doubt, of Buddhist times. My first visit was to Nal, at the foot of the Mōra pass, where, above a small village, diggings made for Colonel Deane in 1897 had brought to light a mass of fine Graeco-Buddhist relievos. These had been excavated from fine Stūpas or shrines by local Pathāns without proper supervision or guidance; but, at least, they were safely lodged in the Calcutta Museum. Much regrettable damage and loss have been caused, before and since, in tribal territory and elsewhere along the Peshawar border, by 'irresponsible' digging for remains of that Hellenistic sculptural art which once adorned all Buddhist sanctuaries of this region (Fig. 4). How destructive such digging usually was and how often much of the spoil, when sold to amateur collectors, was ultimately scattered or destroyed, is a story too sad to be told here.

The site near Nal showed grievous signs of such exploitation (Fig. 5)—small fragments of relievos could still be picked up among shattered ruins on the surface. But it proved a pleasing example of the care with which those old Buddhist monks knew how to select sacred spots and place their monastic establishments by them. A glorious view down the fertile valley to Thāna, picturesque rocky spurs around, clumps of firs and cedars higher up, and the rare boon of a spring close by—all combined to give charm to the spot. Even those who do not seek future bliss in Nirvāṇa could fully enjoy it.

Then up steep rocky slopes, where walls of old monastic quarters cling to narrow terraces or nooks in the crags, we climbed to the ruins of Kāfir-kōṭ, the 'Heathens' Castle'. It proved the site of one of those ancient villages which evidently had been built for security on difficult ridges and hill-tops; their remains abound in these parts. The rough but carefully set slabs of stone could, of course, be obtained on the spot. Yet the labour involved in constructing the terraces that support them, as well as the always massive walls of the quarters, must have been immense compared with the actual accommodation. How an adequate supply of water could be got at such places is somewhat of a puzzle—unless 'desiccation' supplies a solution.

This day's work also included the start of our survey operations from Dosillo-sar, a high point on the range to the east about 4,500 feet above sea-level. It gave us the first close view over the nearest portions of the Swāt valley now ruled by the Miāngul. Finally we clambered up and down the watershed towards Bunēr until we reached the Mōra pass, a narrow gap on the rocky crest. It was a day of arduous but instructive toil, and to my relief it showed that my two Pathān assistants, Tōrabāz Khān, of the Survey, and 'Abdul Ghafūr, the Sapper Naik, new to my ways as they both were, were men of the right stuff.

On the 12th, a day of threatening clouds and occasional drizzling rain, I left my camp near Thāna to make my entry into the Miāngul's dominion. As we passed along the cart road below the low rocky spur which on its terraced slopes bears the densely packed houses of Thāna, I could see how much this emporium of local trade had grown since Lower Swāt was firmly brought under British protec-

4. RELIEVOS FROM RUINED BUDDHIST SHRINES OF SWĀT, PROBABLY OF NAL, REMOVED TO THE IMPERIAL MUSEUM, CALCUTTA.

Relievo in centre of these *disiecta membra* represents Buddha's Nirvāṇa with lamenting disciples, &c. To left figure of a Bodhisattva, to right of Māyā; above legendary scenes; below friezes with garland-carrying putti.

From a photograph kindly supplied by the Superintendent, Archaeological Section, Imperial Museum.

tion. Quite a row of large Sarais and shops, the latter all kept by Hindus, now lined the roadside, and the substantial mansions of the two chief Khāns of the place were to be seen above. It was interesting to note that these rambling residences, with their arcaded verandahs of timber, lacked the defensible towers without which such men of position and means, avowed leaders also, no doubt, of local factions, would not formerly have considered their safety assured. That these and other houses of recent date showed none of the elaborate and tasteful wood-carving that adorns old and far ruder dwellings of headmen in Upper Swāt was obviously a penalty paid for the advance of peaceful civilization.

From the village of Haibat-grām, a couple of miles farther up the main valley, I left the road in a southerly direction in order to visit and survey the fairly preserved ruin of a Stūpa or Buddhist relic tower in the small secluded glen of Tōp-dara. The frontispiece shows this monument of Buddhist devotion, erected like all other Stūpas of this region to enshrine under the solid mass of its masonry some reputed relic of the Enlightened One. The protection that the massive dome and its bases were intended to afford to the bone fragment or other relic of the Buddha had failed, as at almost all Stūpas of the Frontier, to save the sacred deposit from spoliation; for greedy hands, probably long ago, had cut through the south-eastern side of the Stūpa and tunnelled right down the centre to discover and abstract what small articles of precious metal, gems or the like, might have been placed as a votive deposit with the relic.

But otherwise the structure had suffered comparatively little, as the photograph shows; its distance from the nearest inhabited ground had probably saved it from use as a quarry. It was accordingly not difficult to determine the measures of the lowest base, fifty-two feet by forty-six, and of the two receding circular bases upon which rested the dome proper with its drum over twenty feet high and twenty-seven feet in diameter. In some places the shallow pilasters still survived which once adorned all the three bases prescribed by tradition; but the small stonework of which they were built had in general decayed, leaving only matrices, as it were, in the solid masonry of large stone slabs which formed the facing of the Stūpa.

A little above the south-eastern side of the quadrangular Stūpa base, where the position of the stairs leading up to its top was traceable, we found the ruinous remains, overgrown by luxuriant vegetation, of what evidently had been a monastic structure, measuring about a hundred feet square. On each side of an open court four small domed chambers could be made out, which probably had served as quarters. The debris-covered slopes of the gully on either side of the ruins may well hide the completely demolished remains of small Stūpas or shrines such as are found so often at sites of this kind. A massive square tower still rising boldly on the steep hill-side to the south of the Stūpa and some two hundred feet above it may well have served as a safe place of refuge when danger threatened the establishment. The narrow bed passing the foot of the Stūpa base is now dry except when rain falls on the hill-side behind. But the gorge about a quarter of a mile higher up holds a perennial spring, and that probably sufficed for the needs of the small monastic community.

As we made our way back to the road north-eastwards under threatening rain clouds, we passed scattered ruins of massively built structures occupying the crests of small detached spurs and extending over more than a mile. The character of their masonry showed that they belonged to the Buddhist period, like the very numerous dwellings of the same type to be found elsewhere in Lower Swāt. The

5. RUINS OF BUDDHIST SANCTUARY, NAL.

6. SMALL SHRINE AT GUMBATŪNA, ABOVE SWĀT RIVER.

position in which they are always found, commanding easily defended slopes, clearly indicates that regard for security had been a determining factor in their construction. There was no time then for closer examination, and I knew that similar ruins of ancient dwellings awaited us farther on.

Near the village of Jalāla we regained what must always have been, as it now is, the main line of communication up the Swāt valley, and following it beyond the village we soon approached the Landakai spur. The steep rocky faces of this spur descend close to the left bank of the Swāt river and serve as the natural defence and boundary of Bar-Swāt or Upper Swāt. Its foot during the spring and summer months is made quite impassable by the river in flood, and the spur itself must often have been held as a barrier against invading forces, just as it was at the time of the great Pathān rising in 1897. As I rode up the unmetalled zigzag road which had recently been built across the end of the spur to please the Miāngul's desire for modern locomotion, I thought how Alexander's Macedonians may have toiled up these rock slopes. After this barrier is passed the road lies quite open across broad riverine flats and leads to the richest and most populous parts of Swāt.

CHAPTER IV

WELCOME BY AN OLD FRIEND

We reached Kōtah, the first village of the Miāngul's territory and a large place surrounded by rice-fields, in drizzling rain, and felt glad to find camp duly pitched some distance off, outside a small fort of true medieval appearance. Like others along the main route up the valley, it had been recently constructed, visible evidence of the ruler's correct perception of his subjects' still somewhat unsettled allegiance. I was delighted to find myself welcomed there, on behalf of the 'Bādshāh', by Shāh 'Ālam, the nephew of Rāja Pakhtūn Wālī and my former guide and protector in Darēl and Tangīr (Fig. 7). I still remembered with pleasure how well this attractive young scion of the Khushwakt race, ever alert in body and mind, had looked after our safety and comfort when, in 1913, at the start of my third Central-Asian journey, I passed through those alpine valleys to the north of the Indus which his uncle, Rāja Pakhtūn Wālī, had carved into a new kingdom for himself. No European had ever visited them before.

I have had occasion to tell elsewhere the story of the brave fights and unscrupulous intrigues, suggestive of Renaissance times on Italian soil, by which that capable chief had raised himself from the position of a hapless refugee from Chitrāl to that of absolute master of a number of turbulent little republics of Dard race. Shāh 'Ālam, scarcely as yet emerged from boyhood, but possessed of a keen brain and a good native education, was then acting as his uncle's Wazīr. Four years after my visit the newly created dominion came to a sudden end, by methods similar to those which had brought about its rise, through the treacherous murder of Rāja Pakhtūn Wālī in Tangīr. In the course of the same day the Rāja's main castle at Jalkōṭ had been

7. RĀJA SHĀH 'ĀLAM, KHUSHWAKT, NEPHEW OF THE LATE CHIEF OF DARĒL AND TANGĪR.

sacked and burnt, and Shāh 'Ālam obliged to escape with his uncle's wives and children across the mountains to the valley of Kandia.

Two plucky attempts he had since made to assert claims by inheritance over Tangīr and Darēl on behalf of the young sons of the murdered ruler; but both had failed owing to lack of resources wherewith to secure the adequate support of a tribal mercenary force. So Shāh 'Ālam with the two boys had sought refuge with the Miāngul, whose power might yet help to restore the family's fortune. It was a real pleasure to me to see that he had retained his mental and physical activity, and as before I found in him a most congenial and helpful companion on all occasions. I had, therefore, every reason to feel grateful to the Bādshāh for attaching Shāh 'Ālam to me. I was glad, too, to observe that his present quasi-dependent position did not in any way diminish his status with the Swātīs, who call him Shāhzāda (prince) or Rāja; and it was evident that, like a true Khushwakt, he did not take such ups and downs of fortune too much to heart.

Many a good talk we had together on the long tramps that I devoted to ruined 'Gumbats' or domes, *i.e.* Stūpas, and other ancient remains during the next few days. There was much rain during the first two of them, but this did not prevent some interesting surveys. A heavy rain storm during most of the night that followed our arrival at Nawēkala, 'the new castle', of Kōtah, threatened to turn our camping ground into a bog and made me feel very sorry for the Bādshāh's men-at-arms posted as sentries around our tents here as at all subsequent camps. Fortunately they managed to secure 'charpoys' or strung rope cots on which to crouch while keeping their watch. Fortunately, too, I could let the Surveyor and Naik seek shelter within the fort, dark and uninviting as its quarters looked. The rain continued to pour through the greater part of the morning and made it difficult to attend to anything but drainage operations around the soaked tents. Later on, however, I was able to set out, under misty skies and occasional heavy showers, for the 'old mansions' (*māṇrai*). They could be seen crowning a succession of low ridges which descend into the broad valley from the east slopes of the Landakai spur.

On all of them we found ruins of ancient dwellings ranged one above the other on small terraces along the narrow crest of the ridges (Fig. 3). Their characteristic construction—thick walls of undressed but carefully laid stone slabs—left no doubt that they went back to the Buddhist period like the many similar structures I had previously examined near the Malakand and on the slopes of the picturesque hills rising like islands above the fertile plain of the Peshawar valley, the ancient Gandhāra. Almost all these dwellings stood well apart from each other, half a dozen or more rooms adjoining a square keep-like tower. The latter was invariably built solid up to a height of ten to twelve feet from the ground, the entrance having evidently to be reached by a wooden ladder or other contrivance, easily withdrawn in case of attack.

This arrangement, as also the very massive masonry of the walls enclosing the quarters or small outside courts, made it clear enough that defence was the main consideration. The windows piercing the walls of the rooms suggested the same purpose, where they could be traced. They were all very narrow on the outside, like loopholes, but splayed out within to give the maximum of light permitted by such a safeguard. The narrow doorways still showed the square holes where heavy wooden cross-bars had been fitted on the inside. In spite of the heavy debris encumbering most of the interior, it was possible to trace here and there the small neatly walled underground pits which had served for the storage of grain.

There could be no doubt that these defensible structures were here and elsewhere intended to provide safety for their occupants when danger threatened, whether from outside or from local enemies. The construction of such massive dwelling-places, difficult of access and far away from cultivable level ground, must have involved an outlay of labour incomparably greater than that required to build the rubble-and-mud houses that satisfy even the well-to-do among the present Pathān population of Swāt. It was evident, therefore, that such dwellings could have been built only by local headmen and other people of substance. It seemed safe, too, to conclude that conditions of insecurity must have been frequent during Buddhist times, notwithstanding all the pious devotion that prevailed throughout the Swāt region at that period, as the many ruined sanctuaries and the records of our Chinese pilgrims attest.

On the other hand it would be quite wrong to suppose that these defensive towers indicated a particularly bellicose character in the population of this tract, as they do at the present day on certain parts of the north-western borderland, say amongst Afrīdīs or Wazīrs. Against such a mistake I was warned by recollections of the westernmost marches of China proper. There, in Kansu, I had seen not only every village, but every single outlying farm or hamlet, surrounded by high thick walls of stamped clay. But those who tried to protect themselves by these defences of quite impressive appearance were all peaceable Chinese folk—and in scarcely any instance had their formidable walls helped to save them from the devastating hordes of the last great Tungan rebellion. The scarcity of broken pottery among these ruined Swāt mansions was perhaps a more puzzling feature. Was its absence a sign that these defensible structures had served only as places of occasional refuge while their owners in ordinary times preferred to dwell lower down nearer to water and their lands? Only the systematic excavation of more than one such site could furnish a definite answer.

The night brought more heavy rain, and when on the following morning it cleared somewhat and a move up the valley became possible, it was up a 'high road' resembling a wide channel of liquid mud that we tramped. Still, the three miles thus covered to near Guratai village were easier going than the wide belt of flooded rice-fields between the village and the point where the Swāt river had to be crossed for a visit to ruins reported on the right bank. As throughout the main portion of the great valley the river was flowing in several branches. The principal one, about a hundred and fifty yards wide, was far too deep to be forded on horseback, in spite of the early season. So we took to a raft of goat-skins, steered by a strong-armed old ferryman, which brought us in safety to the opposite bank (Fig. 8). But the frail contrivance could carry only five people and was at each crossing swept by the swirling river over half a mile down stream. So it took some time before our whole party, including the escort, was collected and a move made across other boggy rice-fields to the small hamlet of Gumbatūna.

As its name, the 'domes', had suggested, we found there a whole group of ruined Stūpas nestling between two small spurs which an offshoot of the high range to the north sends down to the river. This sheltered nook in the hill-side immediately overlooks the track that here leads along the right bank of the river and must have formed an attractive place of pilgrimage for the pious. On an artificially widened plateau above the alluvial flat rises a large but badly injured Stūpa, resembling that of Tōp-dara in size and type (Fig. 9). By the side of it a high and massive square base is to

8. RAFT CROSSING SWĀT RIVER TO RIGHT BANK BELOW GUMBATŪNA.
Bīr-kōṭ hill rising above left bank.

9. RUINED BUDDHIST STŪPA AND SANCTUARY, GUMBATŪNA.
Rice-fields and beds of Swāt river in distance.

be seen, which may once have carried a shrine or Vihāra, while the remains of two much broken Stūpas of smaller size could be traced near the foot of the big one. All these structures had been burrowed into a long time ago for 'treasure' and probably more than once; thus the large Stūpa, besides having its square base tunnelled into from the west, showed a wide shaft sunk down the centre from the top. Yet in spite of all the ravages of time and the hand of man, parts of the drum and dome still retained layers of the hard cement-like plaster that probably once covered the outside of all such pious monuments.

Rain forced us later to seek shelter in the mosque. The ancient walled-up terrace on which it stands rises some fifty feet above the Stūpa plateau and was once, no doubt, occupied by monastic buildings, like the neighbouring ground on which the hovels of the hamlet are built. Fortunately a small circular shrine, in a narrow ravine a short distance above the mosque and near a fine spring, had fared better. The little rotunda, with an interior diameter of about fifteen feet, still carries a rather flat dome on its high massive walls (Fig. 6). The debris-filled interior may well hide remains of the stucco images of Buddhist divinities that probably once stood in the shrine. The existence of a spring in this picturesque gully and the fine view right across the wide valley may have had much to do with the selection of this spot by pious tradition as one of the many hallowed by the Buddha's visit to ancient Uḍḍiyana.

Just as I stood by the spring the sun came out at last and illuminated a beautiful landscape. Across the wide flood-beds of the river to the south-west the rugged hill of Bīr-kōṭ rose boldly in striking isolation (Fig. 8); it was soon to become a familiar landmark for us all and for me one of no small historical interest. Behind it, far away, showed the snow-covered slopes of Mount Ilam, dominating from its height of some 9,200 feet the greater portion of Swāt as well as of Bunēr. The head of the fine dome-shaped peak was hidden by clouds. Twenty-eight years before I had first sighted it from the Bunēr side. I knew that popular legends even now clustered round it, as they did in the old days when Hsüan-tsang, ever eager in his delightfully naïve piety to gather wondrous tales, had heard and recorded them. So I made obeisance to it from afar, with a firm resolve that I should be the first European to tread its heights. And then up the river to the west I caught sight of the glittering dome of the Shankardār Stūpa, a great monument of Buddhist worship, of which reports had reached me many years before.

Having recrossed by raft to the left bank we reached the foot of the far-stretching Bīr-kōṭ hill, whose sheer cliffs drop to a deep channel of the river. Scrambling along the rocky slopes by a difficult foot-path, we made our way to lush meadow land where a lively stream from the south empties itself into the river, and then passed the large village of Bīr-kōṭ. Some distance beyond it I found my camp pitched near the spot where the Miāngul had started constructing a 'Tahsīl', fort, jail, and school—all of them requisites for the consolidation of his rule. Here he had sent his Sipāh-sālār or Commander-in-chief, Aḥmad 'Alī Khān, to await me. With his personal bodyguard of some thirty well-equipped men, he was to look after me throughout my wanderings. And a most pleasant and obliging protector this active and keen-witted warrior proved to be (Fig. 37).

He had fought hard in the Miāngul's cause, as more than one scar on his lithe body showed. But now that aggression from outside had ceased, his chief task was to tour extensively through his master's dominions, to see that the newly built forts at all the important points were properly garrisoned, and in general to show that the ruler, besides a quick brain and inherited spiritual authority, was endowed also with a sword-arm, ready to enforce his rule. May it last long, was my wish, spreading peace in a region greatly favoured by nature and already growing in wealth. Some day the Bādshāh's dominion, including the high alpine valleys of the Swāt Kohistān, may rank as the Kashmīr of the Frontier, to be admired alike for its natural beauties and resources. But for the present I felt quite content to see Swāt passing happily from turbulent faction to settled conditions under a strong 'benevolent tyrant'.

CHAPTER V

BĪR-KŌṬ AND THE RUINS AROUND IT

BĪR-KŌṬ village is delightfully situated below the eastern end of the hill to which, as we shall see farther on, it owes its name. Close to it three large and fertile side valleys unite before debouching towards the river. They descend from that portion of the watershed range which divides Swāt from Bunēr and is crowned by Mount Ilam. Their upper slopes are well wooded with cedars, firs, and pines, and abundance of shrubs and grass clothes the lower slopes, at any rate in spring-time. So I enjoyed something like alpine surroundings during the days that I had to devote to the numerous and important ruins to be found in these valleys. My search for them was greatly facilitated by the very intelligent and active local guide whom I found in young 'Abdul Latīf Khān, the son of the chief Khān and landowner of Bīr-kōṭ; he had joined me as a kind of liaison assistant at the suggestion of Mr. Metcalfe.

'Abdul Latīf was the first youth of Upper Swāt who had received an English education up to the undergraduate standard at the Islamia College of Peshawar. He had successfully passed the departmental examination for enrolment as candidate for a Naib Tahsīldārship, the lowest administrative grade in the Frontier Province. But no vacancy had as yet offered for his probationary employment, and finding time hang heavily on his hands among his less enlightened compatriots beyond the border, he eagerly accepted the chance of making himself useful to a Sāhib under the British Government which he hoped to serve. Fortunately Rāja Shāh 'Ālam, though English is not one of the half-dozen tongues comprised in his linguistic equipment, took kindly to this first product of 'Western education' among the Bādshāh's subjects, and this couple

10. RUINS OF BUDDHIST RELIC TOWERS, SOUTH-WEST OF BĪR-KŌṬ.

of devoted companions (Fig. 37) made it easy for me to keep my finger, as it were, on local feeling and knowledge.

I have not room to describe here in detail all the ancient remains that four long days of riding and scrambling allowed me to survey around Bīr-kōṭ and higher up those picturesque valleys. Nor do I propose to record what I found and examined in proper chronological order. But even brief notes will suffice to show how abundant are the proofs of pious ardour and worldly wealth left by the ancient Buddhist dwellers in this favoured portion of Swāt. When I proceeded up Kandag, the westernmost of those valleys, I found first a pair of large but ruinous Stūpas within easy reach of Bīr-kōṭ (Fig. 10). The size of the bases, from sixty to seventy feet square, and the conspicuous position they occupied made it possible to reconstruct in imagination the imposing appearance that these structures once presented. But in addition to successive diggings for 'treasure' it was clear that quarrying operations for building stones had proceeded here for ages, while during more recent times search for sculptural remains had helped to complete the havoc.

A couple of miles higher up I found the ruins of a large sanctuary with chapels and monastic quarters, known as Kanjar-kōṭe, the 'dancer's mansion', stretching on different levels for some hundred and seventy yards, below frowning cliffs of red sandstone. Here, too, there was evidence of vandal destruction, due to the search for 'Būts', *i.e.* idols, for sale to collectors or dealers in British cantonments. The contrast offered by this wild solitude, a small Thebais, to the smiling green fields below was strangely impressive in the evening.

An architecturally interesting structure known appropriately as Gumbat, the 'dome' (Figs. 11, 12) which rises on the hill-side near a spring some six miles from Bīr-kōṭ, had fortunately fared better. It consists of a cella nearly twelve feet square within, surrounded on all sides by a narrow passage intended for the circumambulation of sacred images that Buddhist worship, like Hindu cult to this day, prescribes. Small windows piercing the massive walls of both cella and passage gave light to the interior. This probably once contained a colossal standing image of the Buddha; for it would be difficult otherwise to account for the great height, close on fifty feet, of the dome surmounting the cella. Its interior, filled to a considerable height with refuse accumulations, was occupied by a Gujar family from the neighbouring hamlet of Bālo, while the passage was utilized to shelter their buffaloes. On terraces close by I was able to trace the position of several small Stūpas, now completely demolished, and to pick up much-decayed little fragments from relievos, which modern searchers for 'idols' had thrown aside in the course of their destructive operations.

Another long day spent in visiting the ruins of a large Buddhist shrine high up in the valley of Amlūk-dara will ever be remembered by me with delight. My visit led me up to the very foot of Mount Ilam, still invested with legendary sanctity, and all the way through charming spring scenery. On the way up I passed at Nawagai a picturesque village nestling around a fine spring which, as ruined walls and terraces in abundance proved, had also served as the centre of an ancient settlement. Copper coins with Greek legends of Bactrian and Indo-Greek rulers and of their Indo-Scythian successors, including the great Kushān kings, were brought to me in numbers as soon as the first offerings of this sort had been rewarded with a couple of small nickel pieces. They all had been picked up on the steep hill-sides above, dotted with massive remains of stone-built houses and towers. The chronological evi-

11. RUINED BUDDHIST SHRINE, GUMBAT, KANDAG VALLEY, SEEN FROM SOUTH-WEST.

12. ENTRANCE AND PASSAGE OF RUINED BUDDHIST SHRINE, GUMBAT, KANDAG VALLEY.

dence that they afforded with regard to a type of ruins so abundant throughout Swāt proved very valuable.

Then we left the good mule road, much improved by the Bādshāh, leading up to the Karākar pass, which I had first approached in 1898 with a reconnoitring patrol of the Bunēr Field Force. As we turned up a verdant side valley, a brisk little stream, fed by the snow-covered heights of Mount Ilam, refreshed the eye. It made me realize, what one is apt to forget on other far more arid parts of the Frontier, the benefit conferred by water even without the human aid of irrigation. The deep-cut lane along which we travelled was lined with rough hedges showing fine primrose-like flowers in full bloom, and the trees hanging low with their branches, though still bare of leaves, helped somehow to recall Devon lanes. Bluebell-like flowers and other messengers of spring spread brightness over the little terraced fields. At one place they formed what looked like a carpet of worship below a large relievo, carved on a detached rock and showing a seated Buddha. The pious zeal of Pathān invaders—Swāt was occupied by Yusufzai clans only in the fifteenth century—has done what without too much trouble it could to deface the sacred image. Yet this rustic object of worship retained its serenity of head and pose.

Where the little valley bifurcates close above the hamlet of Amlūk-dara, the steep fir-clad heights of Mount Ilam came into full view, covered with snow well down from its bold pyramid-shaped top. It is sufficiently far from the high snowy ranges that rise above the Swāt valley farther up to offer an impressive sight both from Bunēr and from the middle portion of Swāt. It is easy to understand, therefore, the veneration which it still enjoys among the scattered Hindus of these regions and the superstitious legends with which Pathān imagination invests it. We have here merely another illustration of the rule that no conquest nor change of religion can ever efface local worship. Who can tell how far back into antiquity this sanctity of Mount Ilam reaches?

And just to delight the archaeologist, there rose against this grand background a big Stūpa (Fig. 13), of carefully constructed masonry and in more perfect preservation than any I had ever seen. It had not been dug into of old for 'treasure', like all the Stūpas I had so far examined. Nor had the 'Būt' hunter, that destructive agent of modern 'civilizing' influences, been yet at work among the half-dozen decayed mounds marking small Stūpas or shrines on the terraces immediately behind it. The large monument still raises its fine hemispherical dome, about seventy feet in diameter, with its stone facing practically intact, to a height of some forty-eight feet including the circular drum. Together with the customary triple base, the lowest a hundred and thirteen feet square, the whole structure attains a height of close on a hundred feet.

I can scarcely be mistaken in the belief that, apart from small votive Stūpas, it is probably the best preserved of all the ancient shrines that Indian Buddhist worship has raised over supposed relics of its hallowed founder. Nothing had fallen but the huge circular stone umbrellas that had once belonged to the 'Tee' above the dome. Four of them now lay in a heap on the square base of the Stūpa. The largest of them measures fully fourteen feet in diameter: to raise it to that height must have been a task worthy of some Egyptian builder. Of two copper coins said to have been found at the site one proved to be an issue of the great Kushān dynasty and the other of the Turkish Shāhis of Kābul, thus respectively indicating the approximate probable dates when the building was constructed and when worship ceased.

13. RUINED BUDDHIST STŪPA, AMLŪK-DARA VALLEY, SEEN FROM SOUTH-EAST.

Note men standing on base and on top of dome.

The survey of this remarkable site, so well chosen by its 'pious founder', naturally took time, and all the while Mount Ilam was gathering fleecy clouds round the bold crags on its head. Soon after we started back the clouds descended from it, and before more than a few miles of the return march had been covered a heavy rain storm broke, accompanied by much thunder and lightning, and drenched us all thoroughly. My escort, however, half a dozen of the Bādshāh's local men-at-arms, were a lusty lot of hardy youths and seemed quite cheerful in spite of their wetting. When regaled by us with tea in camp they let their thin cotton garments dry on their bodies without showing the slightest discomfort.

From Bīr-kōṭ I visited another big Buddhist site, quite as picturesque as that just described and if anything larger (Fig. 14). It lies in a small wooded dale opposite Naji-grām village which is known as Tōkar-dara. Being more easily accessible it has suffered more damage at human hands. But this was amply compensated by the interesting discovery of an elaborately constructed barrage work, immediately below the big Stūpa (Fig. 15). It was obviously intended to secure a permanent supply of water for what, judging from the extensive ruins of monastic quarters, must have been a very large community. The spring which once may have fed it lies far up on the hill-side (Fig. 16). At the same time I found evidence that the reservoir had also been planned for the supply of systematic irrigation to the terraced fields below. It is the first example so far known to me on the Frontier of an ancient engineering work designed for this double purpose. Months would probably be needed for the complete excavation of the ruins higher up; they are thickly overgrown by thorny jungle and include a large quadrangle with monastic quarters. Even confining myself to mere rough survey and photographic work, I found it difficult to do it justice in a day.

A very different and to the Western student a much higher interest attaches to the ruins of the ancient stronghold that crowns the rugged hill rising above the left bank of the river near the village of Bīr-kōṭ. The hill, completely isolated and rising to close on six hundred feet above the riverine flat (Fig. 8), forms a very conspicuous landmark many miles up and down the valley. It is known as the hill of Bīr-kōṭ, and it has given its name, meaning the 'Bīr Castle', to the village below. It is here that I was first able to identify one of the strong places figuring in the Frontier campaign which preceded Alexander's invasion of the Panjāb and which we know must have taken him into Swāt. But before we examine the records of Alexander's historians supporting this location I may briefly describe the results of the examination of the Bīr-kōṭ hill and its remains.

Where the broad spur flanking the Kandag valley on the west approaches the left bank of the river it curves round to the north-east. After descending to a low and broad saddle crossed by the main road up the Swāt valley, it rises again, marked along its crest by a succession of bare rocky 'kopjes', and ends abruptly in the rugged isolated hill of Bīr-kōṭ. This hill is washed at its northern foot by the river and culminates in a bold rock pinnacle, attaining a triangulated height of 3,093 feet, as shown in the sketch-plan (Fig. 17). The hill is roughly crescent-shaped and drops on its convex side towards the river in precipitous rocky slopes, very difficult to climb and in places quite impracticable (Fig. 19). On its concave side, to the south, high unscalable crags fringe the central portion of the hill and culminate in the rock pinnacle above referred to. Towards the south-west the hill runs out in a narrow rocky

14. RUINS OF BUDDHIST STŪPA AND MONASTERY, TŌKAR-DARA, SEEN FROM SOUTH.

15. WALLS OF BARRAGE BELOW RUINED BUDDHIST SANCTUARY, TŌKAR-DARA.

16. VIEW UP TŌKAR-DARA GLEN WITH RUINED STŪPA.

ridge, utterly bare throughout and for the topmost three hundred feet or so of its height very steep. The south-eastern extremity of the hill towards Bīr-kōṭ village is also very steep and terminates in a rocky crest. Where the slope affords room for small terraces, these are covered with the debris of stone walls marking ancient habitations, and with an abundance of potsherds.

Above the highest of these terraces an imposing stretch of wall, massively built of undressed but carefully set stone slabs, rises to a height of close on fifty feet (Fig. 18). It protected the fortified summit of the hill on that side where the natural difficulties of attack were less. At the same time the filling up of the space behind it had considerably enlarged the level area on the hill-top. This imposing wall continues at approximately the same height to the north. It rounds the head of a rocky precipitous ravine running down to the river, and is thereafter traceable, less massive and less well preserved, all along the steep river front. Where the wall reaches the north-western end of the fortified summit it turns for short stretches to the south-east and south.

I was here able to trace remains of small towers or bastions (Fig. 19) on projecting rocky knolls, intended to ward off any attack that might be attempted from the previously mentioned narrow ridge to the south-west. Beyond this I was able to follow the line of the wall only for a short distance; for the hill is at this point faced by sheer cliffs, and no defences were needed to make the summit wholly unassailable from the plain. Here the rocky pinnacle already referred to rises steeply above the level plateau formed by the rest of the hill-top. The sides facing towards the latter bear remains of ancient masonry wherever there was room for walls. Abundant pottery debris strewing the summit and slopes made it clear that this commanding position had been turned into a kind of citadel and occupied for a long time.

The whole of the circumvallated level area on the top, measuring well over two hundred yards in length and more than a hundred yards at its greatest width, was found to be covered with ruined walls marking decayed habitations. A low mound rising above a bastion-like projection at the south-eastern end looked as if it hid a small completely demolished Stūpa. Another at the opposite extremity might also have been taken for a ruined Stūpa, but for the masses of broken pottery that covered it. Most of the decorated potsherds picked up among the debris of the site could, by the types of their incised or relievo designs, be definitely assigned to the Buddhist period.

In view of the great extent of territory over which my surveys were to take me and of the time required for other work, I could not attempt systematic excavation either here or at any other of the ancient sites that I traced. Nor can I detail here the signs of ancient occupation revealed by the examination of even the surface remains. But I may at least briefly mention the curious relics of ancient means of defence that we found while examining the western line of wall. We came there upon numbers of round water-worn stones of different sizes, undoubtedly brought from the river-bed, such as would be used for slings or heavier missiles. In one heap, which a little experimental digging revealed at a small ruined tower, we discovered no fewer than thirty-eight rounds of this antique ammunition.

An assured water-supply added greatly to the advantages of Bīr-kōṭ as a safe place of defence. So long as the hill-top was defended it was practically impossible for an enemy to cut off access to the river. A main branch of it washes the base of the rocky northern slopes, and the steepness of the bluffs overhanging the river at this spot shows that it must have flowed past them for ages. But there were defences on this side of the hill also; for as I descended

Fig. 17.

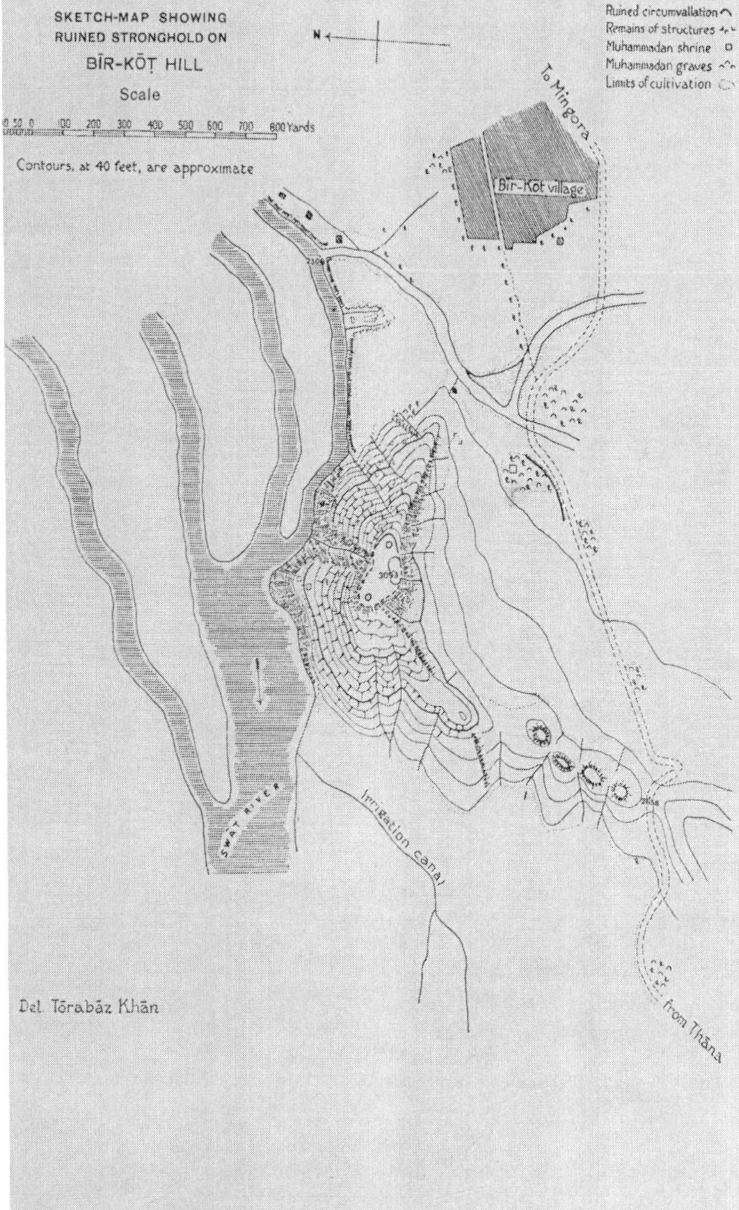
SKETCH-MAP SHOWING
RUINED STRONGHOLD ON
BĪR-KŌṬ HILL
Scale
100 50 0 100 200 300 400 500 600 700 800 Yards
Contours, at 40 feet, are approximate
Ruined circumvallation
Remains of structures
Muhammadan shrine
Muhammadan graves
Limits of cultivation
N
To Mingora
Bīr-Kōt village
SWAT RIVER
Irrigation canal
from Thāna
Del. Tōrabāz Khān

from the hill-top towards the river, in places with difficulty, I noticed remains of old walls and terraces, with abundance of ancient pottery everywhere.

I had been told of two rock-cut passages leading into the hill from above the river, and of the local tradition that they had served to make access to water still more secure. I was shown the entrance to one of them at an elevation of about 180 feet above the river. Once I had passed the low doorway, built of ancient masonry of the type peculiar to structures of the Buddhist period, I found myself in a gallery three feet wide and lined with masonry of the same type. At a height of over ten feet it was vaulted with horizontal courses of cut slabs. I ascended the gallery for only some sixteen yards, to a point where fallen rock partly blocked it. Recesses for a square bolt on either side of the doorway showed that it could be closed from the inside. The exit of another tunnel was found farther to the east and nearer to the cliffs overhanging the river. Here a succession of natural rock fissures appeared to have been utilized by man, for ancient masonry in places lined the rock walls. At a distance of some twenty-five yards ascent became difficult owing to fallen blocks of stone. Whether the two passages meet higher up, as local tradition asserts, could be ascertained only by thorough clearing, which would take time and adequate preparations. But it appeared to me very probable that at least the lower of them, if not both, was intended for the purpose above indicated.

Many coins are found on the top and slopes of the Bīr-kōṭ hill, especially after rain, and attest the great antiquity of the site and its prolonged occupation. Gold or silver pieces are melted down promptly or find their way down through local Hindus to the coin dealers of Rawalpindi or Peshawar. But even so a rapid search made on my behalf at Bīr-kōṭ village produced a large miscellaneous collection of pre-Muhammadan copper coins. The specimens ranged from issues of the Indo-Greek and Indo-Parthian kings and of their Indo-Scythian successors, including the great Kushān rulers of the first centuries A.D., down to the mintages of the 'Hindu Shāhi' dynasty which finally succumbed to the Muhammadan conquest about the close of the tenth century.

Coins of the same early periods are also very frequently found at the numerous sites marked by the remains of Buddhist sanctuaries and ancient habitations around Bīr-kōṭ and in the side valleys that debouch there. They conclusively prove that Bīr-kōṭ must have been the centre of a populous and flourishing tract during the centuries which immediately preceded and followed the time of Christ. It is equally clear that the advantages which the isolated rock-girt hill of Bīr-kōṭ offered, both by its natural defensive strength and its central position on the great highway of Swāt, were probably appreciated long before the period from which the oldest of those coins date.

Only systematic excavation could reveal how far back the earliest occupation of the stronghold dates. But that it already existed when Alexander made his triumphant advance to the Indus and beyond to the plains of the Panjāb, I was soon led to conclude from a careful comparison of the topographical and archaeological facts with the notices of Alexander's historians regarding his operations in this region and the siege of Bazira or Beira in particular.

18. SOUTH-EASTERN PORTION OF FORTIFICATIONS ON BĪR-KŌṬ HILL.

Snow-covered head of Mount Ilam seen in distance.

CHAPTER VI

ALEXANDER'S INVASION OF SWĀT

HERE we may conveniently turn for a moment from the interesting remains of the past which have survived in this fastness to a rapid account of what we learn from the classical records of the arduous campaign that brought Alexander and his hardy Macedonian host into Swāt. In the spring of 327 B.C. Alexander, after two years of strenuous fighting in Bactria and Sogdiana, had crossed the Hindukush towards Kābul. There he strengthened the hold he had previously secured upon this part of what is now Afghānistān, and then set out for the conquest of India.

So far as the country west of the Indus was concerned, this meant only a reassertion of the sovereignty of that Persian empire of which he claimed to be the heir; for ever since the time of the great Darius it had included among its satrapies the present North-West Frontier Province, as well as most of the Indus valley. But under the last weak Achaemenidian 'kings of kings' this sovereignty had probably become very shadowy in the mountainous tracts to the north. This fact, together with the obvious need of securing the flank of his main line of communication, explains why Alexander, on arriving in the upper valley of the Kābul river, led one corps of his army into the hill country to the north, while the rest was to move down into the present Peshawar district and secure the passage across the Indus.

Though we cannot follow the details of Alexander's operations by the river Khōēs, it is certain that they took him for a considerable distance up the large and populous valley of the Kūnar river. Then he crossed the mountains to the east and had more than one hard fight in the territory which the Greek records and geographical considerations combined clearly show to have been the present Bajaur.

The river Guraios, which the Macedonians had to cross before Alexander could lead them into the country of the Assakēnoi, has long ago been proved to be identical with the Panjkōra, the Gaurī of Sanskrit texts. Coming from the mountains of Dīr, it flows past Bajaur on the east and then joins the Swāt river, where it passes through difficult gorges towards the Peshawar plain.

With the passage of the Guraios or Panjkōra, we are told, began the invasion of the country of the powerful nation of the Assakēnoi, and reference to the map shows that this could be no other than Swāt, as has also been long since recognized. The numerical strength of the nation and the size of the territory held by it are sufficiently indicated by what Arrian records of the army gathered by the Assakēnoi to oppose his advance. Yet this host, comprising, we are told, 'two thousand cavalry and more than thirty thousand infantry, besides thirty elephants', did not dare to encounter him in the open and dispersed to their several towns in order to defend them.

From this and the account of the several sieges which followed it seems safe to infer that the Assakēnoi, though a brave race, could not have been addicted to those fierce ways of fighting which make the present Pathān tribes such formidable opponents on their own ground. This conclusion is fully supported by what I have already noted regarding the character of the fortified residences found scattered on the hill-sides of Swāt and the reliance that the ancient inhabitants of Swāt were evidently accustomed to place upon such means of passive defence. It also agrees well with the racial characteristics of those people of Dard stock and language whom we know to have held Swāt before the Pathān conquest and remnants of whom I still found living now in Tōrwāl, the alpine portion of the Bādshāh's territory.

Arrian and Curtius have left us accounts of the protracted operations that were needed for the subjugation of the Assakēnoi. They show clearly that their territory was a large one, extending right away to the Indus. It evidently included, besides the whole of Swāt, Bunēr and the valleys to the north of the latter. These accounts contain details of the places besieged and taken by Alexander; but it had not been possible to fix their position with any assurance so long as by far the greater portion of that extensive area remained inaccessible to antiquarian research.

Only for the initial stages of Alexander's march was definite guidance available, and that was supplied by plain geographical facts. It is certain that in ancient times, as at present, the direct route and the only one of any importance must have led from the Panjkōra through Talāsh and across the easy saddle of Katgala into the wide open valley which thence stretches down to the Swāt river and its strategically important crossing now guarded by the fort of Chakdara. Geographical considerations would further show us that the several fortified towns which Alexander successively besieged and captured were probably situated in the main Swāt valley; for this at all times must, as now, have been the most fertile and populous portion of the territory.

From Arrian, whose account of Alexander's campaign is throughout the most reliable and avowedly based on contemporary records, we learn that Alexander 'marched first to Massaga, which was the greatest city in those parts'. Arrian gives a lengthy account of the siege, which ended with the city's capitulation after a brave defence of four days, after battering engines had been brought up against the walls and the chief had been killed. The reference made to its chief under the name of Assakēnos shows that Massaga was considered the capital. Unfortunately Arrian furnishes no clue to the position of the town; nor are we helped in locating it by Curtius' rhetorical description of its defences, both natural and artificial.

On general grounds I believe that the site of Massaga may probably have to be looked for in Lower Swāt. It must have comprised then, as now, a particularly large proportion of rich land, and the ease with which direct access can be gained from it by a series of passes to the open plain of the Peshawar valley or Gandhāra must have greatly increased its economic and military importance, as it does to-day. It appears very unlikely that Alexander, having been brought by his route from the Panjkōra straight to Lower Swāt, could have carried his operations farther up the valley before securing his rear and the direct line of communication with the rest of his army on the lower Kābul river.

Though the exact location of Massaga cannot be settled for the present, I may briefly refer to two significant facts connected with its siege. One is the mention made of seven thousand Indian mercenaries, brought from a distance, who shared in its defence and after its capitulation made a vain endeavour to regain their homes and in that attempt were exterminated. The employment of so large a paid contingent from outside clearly indicates command of extensive material resources. At the same time it shows that the organized defence which the settled population of ancient Swāt opposed to Alexander was of a very different character from that with which a modern invader of tribal Pathān territories on the North-West Frontier has to reckon, as illustrated by the severe fighting on the Malakand in 1905 and 1907 or in the memorable Ambēla campaign of 1862. In the second place it deserves to be noted that, in spite of the valour shown by the defenders, Arrian puts the total loss suffered by the besiegers at only twenty-five men.

In this cheap price paid for the success we may recognize a proof of the ascendancy which Alexander's highly trained and war-hardened veterans derived from the possession of superior armament; for both Arrian and Curtius bear testimony to the overmastering effect upon the defenders of the besiegers' war engines, including movable towers and powerful ballistae. The remarkable transport feat involved in carrying this ancient artillery and siege train through the mountains, all the way from the Kābul river if not from the Hindukush, is a matter well worthy of the attention of the modern military student interested in these regions.

In tracing the further course of Alexander's operations in Swāt we are fortunately helped by definite archaeological and topographical indications. Arrian's *Anabasis* (IV. xxvii) tells us that Alexander

then dispatched Koinos to Bazira, believing that the inhabitants would capitulate on learning of the capture of Massaga. He further sent Attalos, Alketas, and Demetrios, the cavalry leader, to Ōra, another town, with instructions to invest the town until he himself arrived. A sally made from the latter place against the troops under Alketas was repulsed by the Macedonians without difficulty and the inhabitants driven back within their walls. With Koinos matters did not fare well at Bazira; for its people trusted to the strength of the position, which was very elevated and everywhere strongly fortified, and made no sign of surrender.

Alexander on learning this set out for Bazira. But having come to know that some of the neighbouring barbarians, prompted to this by Abisares, were preparing by stealth to enter Ōra, he first marched to Ōra. Koinos was instructed to fortify a strong position in front of Bazira, to leave in it a garrison sufficient to keep the inhabitants from undisturbed access to their lands, and to lead the rest of his force to Alexander. When the people of Bazira saw Koinos departing with the greatest portion of his troops, they made light of the remaining Macedonians as antagonists no longer equal to themselves and descended to the plain. A sharp encounter ensued in which five hundred barbarians were killed and over seventy taken prisoners. The rest fled together into the town, and were more strictly than ever debarred from access to the land by those in the fortified position.

Subsequently, we are told, when the inhabitants learned of the fall of Ōra, they lost heart and at the dead of night abandoned the town.

In my opinion, the convergent evidence of position, remains, and name enables us to locate Bazira with confidence at the ancient stronghold marked by the ruins on the Bīr-kōṭ hill. To take the topographical indications first, it is clear that Alexander, having made himself master of Lower Swāt, had necessarily to turn his attention next to this strong place of the 'Bīr Castle', which lay quite close to what nature has made the great highway up the Swāt valley. The Bīr-kōṭ hill exactly answers the description Arrian gives of the position of Bazira 'which was very elevated and everywhere strongly fortified'. It is easy to understand why, in spite of the impression which the preceding capture of Massaga must have produced, no rapid success could be gained there by the force under Koinos.

It is equally clear why Alexander, while himself marching upon Ōra, situated higher up the valley as we shall see, was content, instead of attempting a direct siege of Bazira, to leave a small portion of Koinos' troops behind for the purpose of masking the fastness. Considering its great natural strength, nothing less than an arduous and protracted siege could hold out promise of success. It was, moreover, a position from which it was easy for Alexander's opponents to block the main route leading up the Swāt valley and thus to interfere with any operations that Alexander might wish to carry out in that direction. Hence the order to Koinos 'to fortify a strong position in front of Bazira' and 'to leave in it a garrison sufficient to keep the inhabitants from undisturbed access to their lands'. Where that fortified camp is likely to have stood, it is impossible to state with any certainty. Elevated ground near the point where the streams from the Kandag and Karākar valleys

19. RUINED TOWERS AT NORTH-WESTERN END OF BĪR-KŌṬ HILL.

Swāt River seen below in left corner.

20. WALLS CROWNING CREST OF HILL, RĀJA GIRĀ'S CASTLE, UḌE-GRĀM.

On highest point ruins of tower known as 'Takht'.

meet close above Bīr-kōṭ village might well have served the tactical requirements.

Turning to the philological side, it is very easy to prove that the modern name of *Bīr-kōṭ*, 'the castle of Bīr', preserves in its first part the direct phonetic derivative of the ancient local name which the Greek form *Bazira* was intended to transcribe. The Greek letter ζ was regularly used to render both the palatal media *j* and the palatal semi-vowel *y*, two sounds common to the Indo-Aryan and Dardic languages, but not known to the Greek alphabet, and vice versa. Of this we have conclusive evidence in the Greek transcriptions of indigenous names on the coins of rulers belonging to this very region and period. Thus two Indo-Scythian rulers whose coins are found with exceeding frequency at sites of Swāt are known as Azes and Azilizes from the Greek legends on their coins, while the Indian legends on the reverse call them *Aya* and *Ayiliśa*. With the same ease the gradual phonetic change of the restored indigenous form **Bajira* or **Bayira* into **Baira* and then into *Bīr* is accounted for by well-known phonetic laws which govern the development of all Indo-Aryan languages from their ancient into their modern forms and are likewise plentifully illustrated in the related Dard languages. The addition of the designation *kōṭ*, 'castle, fort' (Sanskrit *koṭṭa*), to the name is readily understood, the term *kōṭ* being in general use throughout the North-West of India and in the valleys beyond, whatever the language spoken.

A striking confirmation of the location of Bazira at Bīr-kōṭ and of the derivation of the modern name of the latter is supplied by Curtius. His account, very brief, of the operations that followed those in Bajaur tells us that Alexander 'having crossed the river Khoaspes left Koinos to besiege an opulent city—the inhabitants called it Beira—while he himself went on to Mazaga'. There is good reason to believe that in the Khoaspes we have to recognize either the Swāt river designated by the Iranian form of its ancient Sanskrit name, *Suvāstu*, or else its tributary, the Panjkōra. Though Curtius, by a manifest error, such as frequently occurs in his rhetorical narrative, makes the siege of Beira simultaneous with, instead of subsequent to, that of Mazaga (Massaga), yet the reference to Koinos makes it certain that the *Beira* he mentions is the same as Arrian's Bazira. In this form of the name we have obviously but another attempt to reproduce the indigenous **Bajira* or **Bayira.*

Having thus collated the classical records just detailed with the results of our survey on and around the hill of Bīr-kōṭ, I felt encouraged to hope that with the firm footing here gained I might now be able to clear up the remaining antiquarian questions connected with Alexander's frontier campaign.

21. RUINED BUDDHIST STŪPA, ASCRIBED TO KING UTTARASENA, SHANKARDĀR.

In foreground sunk road cut through outer base of Stūpa.

CHAPTER VII

PAST KING UTTARASENA'S STŪPA

On the morning of March 19th, rendered bitterly cold by a violent wind which had blown all night, I dispatched my camp from Bīr-kōṭ village to Uḍe-grām higher up the main valley. There was much of interest to observe on the road. Only a couple of miles beyond Bīr-kōṭ I came to the great Stūpa of Shankardār (Fig. 21); I had already heard of this huge pile in 1897 and had even been able to catch a distant glimpse of it through my glasses from the top of the Landakai ridge. I found it, alas, in a state of sad ruin. It rises at the very foot of a bare rocky hill just where the highway skirts it. Probably, in consequence of this, it has suffered terrible damage; for the whole village of Shankardār close by, and perhaps others farther away, had utilized the material offered by this convenient quarry.

All round the two lower bases not only the well-carved facing stones but also the greater portion of the interior masonry had been removed. Through what remained of the lowest base the Bādshāh's new road had been cut. The havoc thus wrought made it impossible to determine the dimensions of the ground plan; on the other hand the destruction of the bases seemed to increase the impression created by the height of the Stūpa. From the rough measurements taken the diameter of the dome appeared to be about sixty-two feet, which is somewhat less than that observed at the Stūpa of Amlūk-dara, and the total height over ninety feet from the level of the road. These two large Stūpas were very similar in their architectural features and in the decorative element introduced by the insertion between the fine white facing slabs of little columns of black stones. A big cutting made into the dome from the north-west showed that treasure-seekers had been tempted to work here long ago. But the mass and solidity of the masonry seem to have defeated their efforts, and the central deposit may still be intact.

A special interest attracted me to this ruined pile; for there could be little doubt that it was identical with the Stūpa whose construction a local tradition recorded by Hsüan-tsang attributed to Uttarasena, an ancient king of 'Wu-chang-na' or Swāt. It was believed to cover the share which the king had received of the relics of the Buddha's body in accordance with the Master's own command preceding Nirvāṇa. This location of Uttarasena's Stūpa is clearly indicated, as Colonel Deane recognized long ago, by the position which Hsüan-tsang quite correctly assigns to it. He describes it as east of the Swāt river, at a distance of some sixty *li* or twelve miles south-west of the town of Mêng-chieh-li, marked, as we shall see, by the present Manglawar.

A little farther on I had the great satisfaction of coming upon a striking instance of the accuracy that usually characterizes the records of my Chinese patron saint. He tells us in the 'Memoirs' of his travels of a huge rock, shaped like an elephant, close by on the bank of the river. Tradition saw in it the body of the white elephant that had brought the precious relics for the king; falling dead at this spot it had been miraculously turned into stone. It was easy to recognize this rock at a point less than half a mile beyond the Stūpa, where we passed close below cliffs dropping precipitously to the road before the village of Ghalagai. A projecting part of the rock face (Fig. 22), when seen from a short distance, shows a very curious resemblance to the head and trunk of an elephant. Here, just as if to prove the veneration with which pious eyes used to look up at it, I found the head of a roughly cut relievo image, evidently that of a Buddha, emerging above rock debris. Muham-

22. ROCK FACE RESEMBLING ELEPHANT'S HEAD, NEAR GHALAGAI.

23. ROCK-CARVED IMAGE OF KING, IN GROTTO ABOVE STŪPA, SHANKARDĀR.

madan orthodox zeal had taken care to heap up the latter and do serious damage to the rock-cut head.

An interesting rock-carving some fifty yards farther on had fortunately fared somewhat better, owing to its less exposed position. There a small natural grotto, some forty feet above the road, could be reached with some difficulty by clambering over narrow ledges on the steep face of the cliff, and in it I was shown a remarkable relievo carved from the rock (Fig. 23). The group, about four feet high altogether, had also suffered from iconoclast hands. But in the middle, on a pedestal supported by lions, I could still clearly recognize a bearded figure standing, flanked on either side by smaller much damaged relievo images. The flame halo rising from the shoulders and the dress of the central figure leave no doubt that a royal personage is intended. The costume comprises a long coat falling over bulging trousers stuck into top-boots, and a kind of pelisse or mantle hanging from the shoulders. It is of distinct interest; for it shows such close resemblance to the dress in which the Indo-Scythian rulers of the great Kushān dynasty are represented on their coins and rare sculptures that the relievo is clearly of approximately contemporary origin. Evidently the artist commissioned to raise this modest monument to the memory of pious King Uttarasena represented him in the habiliments of the rulers of his own time, who still retained on the Indian frontier the heavy costume brought from their Central-Asian homeland.

In the course of the next six miles we passed a succession of large villages, all nestling along the foot of bare hill spurs, while towards the river their fertile alluvial land, all used for rice cultivation, stretched in a wide belt. It was easy to see from the number of little shops by the roadside (Fig. 35) that the Hindu traders who almost exclusively keep them could make good profits not only as agents for the export of rice to the plains—a flourishing trade—but also out of the active local demand for manufactured goods from India. But the total absence of gardens and fruit-trees in this fertile and well-watered valley was striking.

It was a sad illustration, seen also elsewhere in Swāt, of the effects of the surviving Pathān custom of *wēsh*, which requires that all land held by a tribal sub-section shall change hands among the different families that compose it at short intervals, usually of four or five years. Such a custom, while significant enough of the democratic spirit prevailing among Pathān tribes, is evidently not calculated to encourage the planting of trees or gardens by those whose tenure of the land would end in a few years. I was told that the Bādshāh was trying hard to wean his subjects from this custom, and as the climate of Upper Swāt is admirably adapted for the growing of fruits of all sorts, their sweetness when once tasted by young and old will, I hope, facilitate his benevolent efforts.

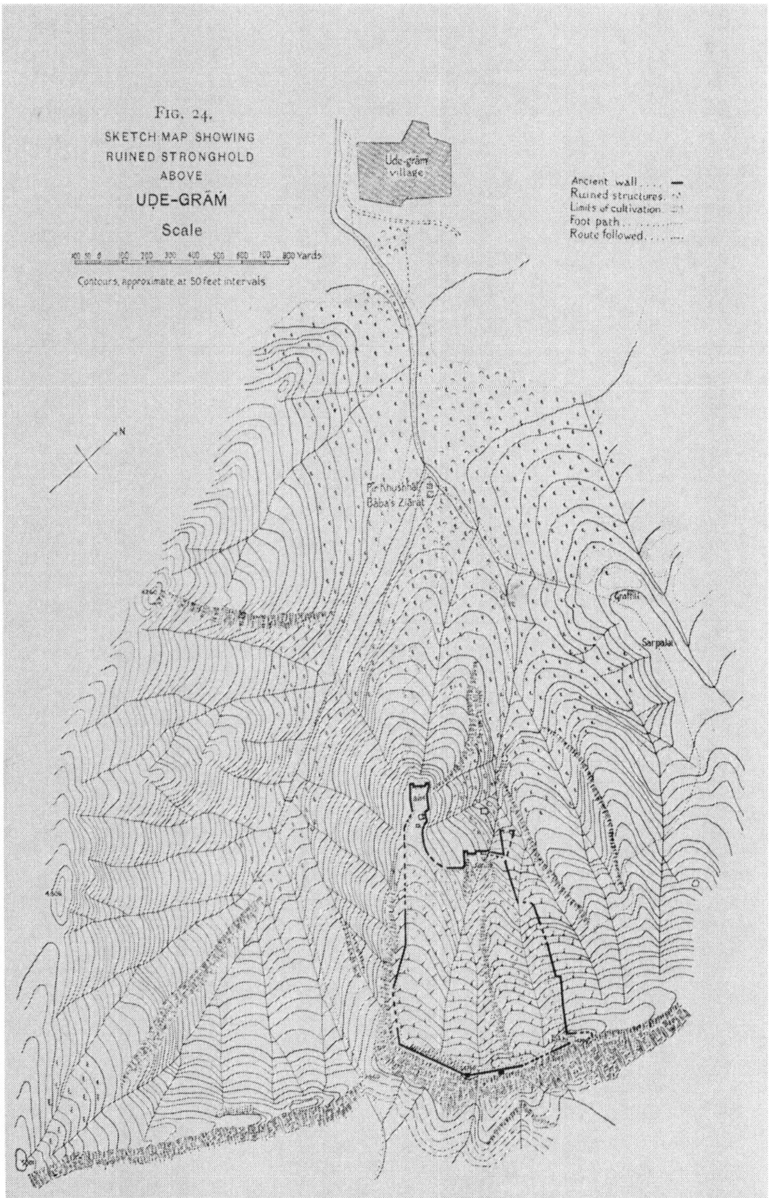

FIG. 24.
SKETCH-MAP SHOWING RUINED STRONGHOLD ABOVE UḌE-GRĀM

CHAPTER VIII

UḌE-GRĀM AND ITS ANCIENT FASTNESS

UḌE-GRĀM, where we halted, proved to be a large place with over four hundred households, and pleasant was the spot where our tents were pitched between the Bādshāh's fortified 'Tahsīl' and the lower edge of a wooded alluvial fan. But what prolonged my stay there and made it fruitful was the unexpected discovery of a large and obviously very ancient mountain fastness on the rugged hill range that rises above Uḍe-grām and the neighbouring villages on the eastern side of the valley. Imagine a huge ribbed scallop-shell turned with its broad edge upwards and its narrow mouth resting on gentle alluvial ground: thus, without sketch-plan (Fig. 24) or photographs, might some idea be conveyed of the peculiar hill formation that here had offered a natural stronghold in times when there were no fire-arms to interfere with safety in a place completely commanding its approaches. The site, known to the local Pathāns as 'King Girā's Castle', was difficult enough to explore—even without the fear of stones or other missiles from above. It cost us two days of stiff climbing along precipitous rock faces and along lines of walls that were carried in places over almost impossible slopes. But it was well worth the labour and fatigue.

Passing up the alluvial fan above mentioned one enters an amphitheatre of steep rocky spurs converging into a well-wooded little valley (Figs. 25, 26) and closed at the back by the serrated crest of the hill range, fully 2,000 feet above Uḍe-grām. Where this serrated crest, nowhere more than about twenty yards wide and in places almost a knife-edge, overlooks the fertile side valley of Saidu, nature, for hundreds of yards, had provided absolutely impregnable defences; for the crest falls away on that side in sheer vertical rock walls and in places forms cornices actually overhanging them from above (Fig. 20). Where a bare narrow spur on that side might bring assailants within reach of a stretch of rock wall that bold climbers could attack with some chance of success, a strong bastion had been built out over projecting cliffs to defeat the attempt. But even while keeping to the line of the crest itself (Fig. 27) I found progress distinctly difficult over certain stretches of this narrow and slippery ground. Yet even over these the line of the ancient wall could be traced. One could hardly think without distress of the labour involved in its construction, at this height and along the difficult rib-like spurs below. The amount of human toil and suffering must have been out of all proportion to the structural remains that have survived the effects of time and of insecure foundations on precipitous slopes.

Along that almost unassailable crest the ancient wall runs for close on eight hundred yards. At its southern end it overlooks a narrow gully through which, about a thousand feet below, a steep footpath passes, connecting Uḍe-grām with the valley of Saidu. Thence the wall turns to the north-west and on a precipitous rocky spur descends some eight hundred feet to a small and narrow plateau. Defended by massive buttressed walls, this plateau projects like a bastion and guards what was the most exposed point of the fortified area (Fig. 28). From here the circumvallation sweeps in an arc round the hollow to the east. It is then carried down another two hundred and fifty feet or so, here and there over veritable crags, until it strikes a dry torrent bed, narrow and rock-lined, down which the main drainage of the protected area finds its way to the valley. Here the line of wall meets another bold outwork, triangular in shape, which defended the approach from this gully.

Then it runs up on an easterly spur to the other end of

25. VIEW UP SLOPES OF ANCIENT STRONGHOLD ABOVE UḌE-GRĀM.

26. VIEW DOWN TOWARDS UḌE-GRĀM AND SWĀT RIVER FROM CREST OF RĀJA GIRĀ'S CASTLE.

the crest which formed the starting-point of our survey (Fig. 29). In spite of the great steepness of this spur, stretches of the wall, with its massive semicircular buttresses, have here survived in remarkable preservation (Fig. 30). We found it in most places about seven feet thick. The steep slope of slippery rock outside this portion of the circumvallation must have greatly facilitated defence. Even within the wall the slope is so steep that only at a few points was there room for quarters occupying small terraces alongside of it; all these were found in far advanced decay. Yet their masonry had been solid enough, consisting, as in the defences, of carefully packed layers of stone set in hard plaster.

Where the line of wall curving from the west approaches, more than a thousand feet below the crest, the gorge below the triangular outwork already mentioned, we found a fine perennial spring gushing from among the big boulders that fill the bottom of the otherwise dry torrent bed. It was the existence of this spring, the only source of water within the area, that rendered it capable of being used as a place of refuge. There was ample and striking proof of the importance attached to the spring in the massive construction of the defences intended to guard it. The walls on either side descend in double lines into the gorge that holds this precious water, and small bastions or towers had been built to strengthen the defences wherever any bit of easier slope allowed it (Fig. 31). Higher up and also towards the south, wherever the slopes afforded room, ruined walls of houses marked ancient occupation. Their condition of advanced decay, as compared with the remains of Buddhist monastic quarters, &c., in other places, was clear evidence of their great antiquity. Communication over the narrow ledges or ladder-like rock paths leading from terrace to terrace must at all times have been difficult, and the poor women who probably had to do most of the water-carrying no doubt had an extremely trying task.

By the side of the spring, ferns and maidenhair were growing profusely among the sheltered rock recesses. Flowers, too, including true scented violets, found their chance of blossoming in the cool humid shade. With one old willow-tree already in full leaf, they combined to make a picture in pleasant contrast with the grim rocks and crumbling fortifications above. It was a spot that might well pass for romantic, and I wished that the gifted author of *Harilek*, my friend Major Gompertz, had been with me to use it as the scene ready set for one of his clever stories.

As I descended the gradually widening gorge in the evening, I noticed in more than one place carefully walled-up terraces that might once have been the site of fruit gardens or other places of recreation for the inhabitants of that strange stronghold. Now nothing grows on them but thickets of thorny Palōsa trees. The whole area is held sacred to the shrine of holy Pīr Khushhāl Bābā, situated farther down by the side of a lively little rill. So none of the fertile soil near or below this Ziārat, verdant meadow land as it was at this early spring season, may be cultivated. I hoped that the time might come when the superior power, at once spiritual and secular, of the new ruler of Swāt would cause it to be planted with those orchards which the valley sorely needs and which its sub-alpine climate would distinctly favour.

But how could there be gardens or orchards in a land in which, until a few years before, the frequent redistribution of all holdings had remained obligatory under the old tribal law? Not until the Pax Britannica had slowly but steadily made its influence felt up the Swāt river, had it been possible for this land so favoured by nature to recover from the slow decay into barbarism which had already begun when pious

27. VIEW ALONG FORTIFIED HILL CREST, RĀJA GIRĀ'S CASTLE, UḌE-GRĀM.

28. NORTH-WESTERN SPUR WITH BASTION, RĀJA GIRĀ'S CASTLE, UḌE-GRĀM.

Hsüan-tsang came to visit and describe 'the kingdom of *Wu-chang-na*, the Garden'.

Both in the little valley just described and on the alluvial fan descending below it (Fig. 26) one could trace other low crumbling walls of ancient structures amidst the thick growth of scrub and thorny jungle. Such remains were particularly numerous at the foot of the spur that bears the south-western flanking line of wall. Here a succession of walled-up terraces, all once, no doubt, occupied by houses, orchards, or gardens, afforded the easiest approach to the fortified area. And this explains why the small plateau that forms the end of that flanking wall had been turned into a particularly massive bastion (Fig. 28), which still rises in places to a height of over twenty feet. Over most of the ground near the walls and below them broken pottery of distinctly ancient type was to be found in plenty. Yet in view of the extreme steepness of the slopes above, it seemed to me hard to believe that the quarters within the walled area were regularly occupied except in times of danger. On the other hand it is improbable that the construction of extensive defences on such difficult slopes would have been undertaken except for the purpose of assuring a safe retreat for the inhabitants of an important locality.

For such a locality the mouth of the valley, where it opens towards Uḍe-grām village, would have afforded ample room. It is now covered with extensive Muhammadan burial grounds and sacred groves belonging to the Ziārat that is here venerated as the resting-place of holy Pīr Khushhāl Bābā. Finds brought to me, consisting of the fragment of a small Graeco-Buddhist relievo, an inscribed Buddhist seal, and coins of the Indo-Scythian rulers, pointed clearly to the early occupation of this ground. But owing to its sacred character systematic search would have been difficult, even if time had been available. Pious tradition recognizes in the saintly hero and martyr, Pīr Khushhāl Bābā, the leader of the Faithful in the army of Maḥmūd of Ghazna, who after a long siege took 'King Girā's fortress' from the last infidel king of Swāt.

Maḥmūd of Ghazna, the great invader from the Afghān highlands, who first laid the north-west of India open to conquering Islām, is the oldest historical figure to which popular legend on the Frontier reaches back. The traditional location of one of his exploits at 'King Girā's Castle' would therefore suffice to prove the high antiquity that popular belief ascribes to the site. But indications furnished by the classical accounts regarding the direction of Alexander's operations beyond Bazira, and considerations connected with the name that I shall presently set forth, soon suggested to me the question whether we should not look here for the probable location of Ōra.

In order to examine this question we must revert to what we have already learned from Arrian about Ōra. Alexander, after the capture of Massaga, had sent certain of his commanders to that town with instructions to invest it until he himself arrived. A sally made from the place against a portion of the investing force commanded by Alketas 'was repulsed by the Macedonians without difficulty and the inhabitants driven back within their walls'. Alexander himself first set out for Bazira, but subsequently was induced to proceed straight to Ōra on learning of a move among the neighbouring barbarians, instigated by Abisares, to reinforce its defenders.

Unfortunately, Arrian's further brief mention of Ōra supplies no topographical or other local hint. He merely tells us that 'he took the town on the first assault against its walls and secured the elephants left behind there'. Nor does Curtius' account help us. He mentions, indeed, a place Nora, to which Alexander dispatched a force under

29. RUINED FORTIFICATIONS ON EASTERLY SPUR OF RĀJA GIRĀ'S CASTLE, ŪḌE-GRĀM, SEEN FROM BELOW SPRING.

Polysperchon after the capture of Mazaga, and this has been generally assumed to be the same as Arrian's Ōra. But all that we are told about it is that Polysperchon 'defeated the undisciplined multitude which he encountered and pursuing them within their fortifications compelled them to surrender the place'. Since the textual records fail us, we must feel all the more grateful for the guidance afforded by the confident location of Bazira at Bīr-kōṭ.

That Ōra lay higher up the Swāt valley than Bazira may safely be concluded from two observations. One is the reference made to Abisares. We know from his very name, the Sanskrit Abhisāra, and from other Greek notices in connexion with Alexander's further campaign, that this chief ruled over the territory on the left bank of the Indus where it faces the upper portion of the main Swāt valley. If Ōra was to be reinforced or relieved by tribesmen acting under Abisares' instructions or impulse, it was obviously because its position farther up the main valley allowed of access to it from that side without interference by the Macedonians who had already secured Lower Swāt. We are led to the same conclusion by the fact that Alexander, as we have seen, ordered Koinos, who stood before Bazira, to join him for the attack upon Ōra with the main portion of his force, while taking care to have Bazira masked by the remainder. The position occupied by Bīr-kōṭ on the main line of communication leading up the Swāt valley explains the necessity of this measure and at the same time clearly shows that Ōra lay beyond it.

These considerations, combined with the general geographical features, must lead us to look for Ōra higher up the main Swāt valley and at some point which the presence of ancient remains would definitely indicate as having been occupied by a fortified town of some importance. Now Upper Swāt above Bīr-kōṭ shows, at the present day, a number of large places which might be called towns, such as Mingaora, Manglawar, and Chārbāgh, all on the left bank of the river. But at none of these, apart from Uḍe-grām, did I succeed in tracing definite evidence of ancient fortification. Nor did I hear of such remains at any of the large villages to be found near the right bank. This quasi-negative fact would by itself suffice to draw our attention to the ruined stronghold above Uḍe-grām as the probable position of Ōra. But more reliance, I believe, can be placed on the evidence which is supplied by the name *Uḍe-grām* itself.

As regards this name it must be explained in the first place that it is certainly a compound of which the second part is the term *grām* (Sanskrit *grāma*), 'village'. This is well known to most Dardic languages and very common in old local names of Swāt, being attached to the special designation just as the word *kōṭ*, 'fort, castle', is in other names. The first part *Uḍe-*, also heard as *Uḍi-*, is pronounced with that cerebral consonant *ḍ* which to European ears, in classical times as now, always sounded like an *r* and often undergoes that change to *r* in modern Indian and Dardic languages. Thus the temptation is great to recognize in Arrian's Ὦρα the Greek rendering of an earlier form of this name *Uḍe-*, and to derive this name itself from the ancient Sanskrit name of Swāt, *Uḍḍiyana*. The phonetic changes that such a derivation assumes in the history of the name can all be fully accounted for by well-known rules affecting the transition of Sanskrit words into later Indo-Aryan forms.

Arrian's account of the impression produced among the Assakēnoi by the fall of Ōra is a proof of the importance attaching to the place, and may perhaps also reflect the reliance that had previously been placed upon its natural strength. We have already seen that the people of Bazira

30. WALL ON EASTERLY SPUR, RĀJA GIRĀ'S CASTLE, UḌE-GRĀM.

31. RUINED TOWER OF OUTWORK GUARDING SPRING, RĀJA GIRĀ'S CASTLE, UḌE-GRĀM.

on hearing of the fall of Ōra abandoned their town. But in addition we learn that 'thus the other barbarians, too, did; leaving their towns, they all fled to the rock in that country called Aornos'. To Arrian's description of that mighty mass of rock and to his account how the fame of its impregnability fired Alexander with the ardent desire to capture it, I shall recur when relating my subsequent search for it by the banks of the Indus.

In the Swāt valley itself, it is clear that the capture of Ōra had brought Alexander's operations to a triumphant conclusion; for Arrian's narrative shows us that, after establishing Macedonian posts at Ōra and Massaga, as well as at Bazira, to guard the country, the conqueror turned south to the Peshawar valley. There he was to establish his junction with the division of the army that had preceded him down the Kābul river, and then to carry his campaign farther east to the Indus.

CHAPTER IX

AT THE BĀDSHĀH'S CAPITAL

It was not the survey of the ruins of 'Rāja Girā's Castle' alone that made my stay at Uḍe-grām an exceedingly busy one. In the close vicinity there were other ancient remains to be visited, clearly proving the past importance of the place. On skirting the foot of the hill-side towards Gōg-dara, another large village, scarcely more than a mile away, I found a group of Buddhist relievos carved from a rock by the roadside, including a colossal seated Buddha; they had, of course, all suffered serious damage at the hands of iconoclasts. High up in the bare stony gully that runs down to Gōg-dara a little spring issues from a rock fissure, and on a terrace above it rise the ruins of a Buddhist monastery, known as the 'quarters of Hasan'. The building, which included rows of small vaulted rooms as well as several long narrow chambers, had originally been of more than one story. But though the top story had fallen, the apartments in the two below seemed to need but little repair to make them once more habitable for pious mendicants. The fair preservation of these monastic quarters was in striking contrast with the far advanced decay of the buildings within the hill fastness above Uḍe-grām, and thus bore witness to the great antiquity of the latter. The Stūpa round which the devotion of the monkish community and of its pious supporters once centred had long ago been wrecked.

There was also a large mound, indicating prolonged occupation in ancient times, to be examined amidst the fields close below the present Uḍe-grām. It appeared to be a remnant of an extensive area that had once been inhabited and was now probably buried under alluvial deposits or turned into terraced rice-fields. Finds of early coins, moreover, were said to be frequent here. But in

32. HOUSES OF MINGAORA, SEEN FROM SOUTH.

33. TOWERS, OFFICE QUARTERS, AND DWELLINGS, SAIDU.

spite of all these vestiges of antiquity I was glad to leave Uḍe-grām on March 23rd and reach Saidu, the hereditary seat of the Bādshāh; for I felt it advisable to meet without further delay the remarkable chief whose rise had given me access to this fascinating and hitherto forbidden land.

It was under a brilliantly clear sky that we moved up the main valley past Bālo-grām and Kambar to where two large side valleys descending from the watershed towards Bunēr meet and debouch upon the Swāt river. As we approached the great bend of the latter, we came into view of the great glittering snowy peaks above Mankiāl, which, far away to the north, dominate the uppermost course of the river. In the open bay that the valley forms at this junction there lay before us Mingaora, now the largest place in Upper Swāt, quite a little town with its closely packed flat-roofed houses (Fig. 32). Fields green with the young grass of spring set it off pleasantly against the dark rugged spur of Shamēlai, which here juts out boldly into the main Swāt valley and forces the river to change abruptly from the southerly course that it has so far maintained and to flow almost due west.

Mingaora, favoured by its situation near the present political centre of Upper Swāt and of easy access from all directions, seemed to be on the way to rivalling Thāna as a modest commercial emporium. I found the long narrow lanes of its Bāzār packed not only with people from Upper Swāt, but also with 'Kohistānīs' from Tōrwāl and the other high valleys on the headwaters of the Swāt river. They were easily recognizable by their heavy Dard features and their coarse woollen cloaks, as were also the rarer and far more uncouth figures from Jalkōṭ, Palōs, and other turbulent little republics in the still inaccessible Kohistān of the Indus gorges.

It was interesting to note the quantity of good wood-carving displayed on the doors and in the interiors of most of the shops (Fig. 34). Among crowded designs of a florid geometrical type I recognized graceful acanthus scrolls and other floral motifs frequently met with in Graeco-Buddhist sculpture. It was welcome proof that the influence of Hellenistic art, to which the relics of ancient Swāt so strongly bear witness, had not been altogether effaced by the flood of barbaric invasion. I was soon to find far more distinct traces of it surviving in the domestic architecture of Tōrwāl, whose alpine seclusion had helped to protect remnants of the old Dard population of Swāt.

In Swāt, as elsewhere on the Frontier, there is little hope that modern Western influence will serve to revive the artistic elements in the crafts of the country. But here, too, it must lead to improvements in the material conditions of life. And I found welcome evidence of this in the well-stocked store newly opened by the Bādshāh's administration. It seemed intended to bring within easy reach of the people not only useful agricultural implements, materials for the safe transport of produce, and the like, but also some civilized luxuries such as books and writing materials. A wooden box was hung outside for the reception of letters, which at suitable times would be sent on to the British post office at Thāna, visible proof that contact with the outside world was also to be encouraged.

There were several ruined Stūpas to be visited near Mingaora, all at the foot of the hill-sides overlooking the streams which meet there from the side valleys of Saidu and Janbil. But none of them were comparable in size to the great Stūpas that I had visited near Bīr-kōṭ. Stripped by vandal hands of their facing stones to provide convenient building material, they had all decayed into shapeless conical mounds. So their examination did not take much time, and the frowning cliffs on the crest of King Girā's Castle were still

34. DOOR OF SHOP WITH WOOD-CARVING, MINGAORA.

35. HINDU TRADER'S SHOP, GŌG-DARA.

bathed in full sunshine as I rode up the smiling verdant valley towards Saidu, the hereditary seat of the Bādshāh and now in course of rapid development into the capital of Upper Swāt. Here his holy grandfather, the great Ākhund of Swāt, had lived as a spiritual leader. He, too, like so many holy men in the west, had known how to choose the right spot for pious devotions, while alive, and for local worship thereafter.

Saidu, situated some 3,300 feet above the sea, occupies a delightfully open position at the foot of a wooded spur descending from an outlier of Ilam and dividing two pretty side valleys. From afar, as I made my way up, I could see the features characteristic of the past and present of the site. Amid a cluster of trees and pilgrims' rest houses the gilt-domed structure could be seen which shelters the remains of the holy 'Ākhund' or Teacher. Under his spiritual leadership Swātīs and Yusufzais had for years fiercely resisted Sikh aggression, while Mahārāja Ranjit Singh, the rival 'Buzurg' of the Panjāb, was growing old.

Around, on prominent hill-tops, high towers could be seen, quite medieval in appearance (Fig. 33), designed to offer safe refuge in case of inter-tribal attack or of sudden invasion from the Bunēr side. The need for them was very real in the years when the Miānguls—there were two then—had to carry on a bitter struggle with rivals for secular power, whom jealous neighbours, the Nawāb of Dīr to the north-west and the Nawāb of Amb, my host in 1921, were egging on and supporting in the interests of their own 'forward policy'. Now white-terraced mansions of semi-European style have risen, since the Bādshāh has made himself sole possessor of his grandfather's sacred inheritance and full master of all the land.

Significantly enough a little higher up, above the new residence constructed for the chief's eldest son, stands the

Bādshāh's 'Kār-khāna' or factory. Here clever artificers are at work making fair imitations of Lee-Metfords, quantities of ammunition, and even small guns. No doubt, the Bādshāh may well have need of support of this kind for some time to come. But the Middle School that has been established and a well laid out garden which I passed by the side of the high road as I came up the valley showed that he was not neglecting other elements of stability.

By the side of the chief's own residence, a rambling place with several airy halls and smaller apartments connected by screened galleries, I found a large comfortable tent pitched for my quarters in a newly planted garden. There I was formally welcomed by the Sipāh-sālār Aḥmad 'Alī and his capable elder brother Wazīr Hazrat 'Alī, the Bādshāh's chief executive and judicial officer (Fig. 37). In the evening, when duly refreshed, I had a long talk with the Bādshāh in the modest apartment that serves as his private council chamber. He assured me at the outset of his full acceptance of my programme. I was to be free to extend my tour to any point within his present borders that I might be interested to visit. But he insisted on the hospitable condition that I and my party should continue to be treated as his personal guests, notwithstanding the wish I urged to the contrary in view of the probable length of my tour. What did half a dozen people more or less matter, he retorted with a humorous look in his eye, when he had daily to provide for the entertainment of a couple of hundred guests!

It was very interesting to listen to the Bādshāh's lively talk about the places that he had visited years ago in the course of his Mecca pilgrimage, the holy shrines of Egypt, Palestine, Syria, and Irāq; for though the spiritual interests prompting this voyage were duly emphasized, he had evidently made it the occasion of many shrewd observations on the things of this world. For my own part I had to answer questions about the ancient history of Swāt. I was fortunately able to give him a piece of information that interested him more than accounts of Buddhist sanctuaries and the like, when I told him that the union of Swāt and Bunēr accomplished under his rule had already been duly recorded by the early Chinese pilgrims. To satisfy his curiosity about my Central-Asian explorations I gave Ataullah Khān, his chief Munshi or literatus (Fig. 37), a copy of the Persian abstract account of my second expedition. It had been prepared years ago in the hope that it might help to secure access to the land, alas, still closed for me, of a greater ruler beyond the Indian Frontier.

My first day at Saidu was used, apart from plentiful writing work, for a visit prescribed both by interest and local etiquette to the shrine of the great Ākhund, the Bādshāh's holy grandfather. His tomb rests in a domed pavilion, enclosed by open-work screens of which the old portions show how much skill and taste still survived fifty years ago among the craftsmen of Swāt. By their side some recent gilded additions looked gaudy. The holy Ākhund's tomb attracts throughout the year many pilgrims from all parts of the Frontier between Peshawar and the Hindukush, and the offerings received from them by the shrine are justly believed to constitute a very considerable annual revenue for the saint's family, the hereditary guardians of the tomb. Religious students from Swāt and different neighbouring hill tracts receive instruction in Islamic law as well as bodily sustenance in the 'Jumāt' attached to the shrine. In the large loggia that serves for their instruction I saw some very good wood-carving. I naturally did not fail to deposit my own offering to the saint with the custodians of the shrine.

I visited the magnificent spring, shaded by fine old plane-trees, that issues close to it, and wondered how much it might have helped to attach the holy teacher to this favoured spot during his long life. A visit to the Bādshāh's Darbār hall, a large wooden structure with much good carving on columns and panelled walls, concluded the day's sightseeing within Saidu. Later in the evening the Bādshāh kindly took me in his motor-car down to the river bank past Mingaora and showed me the road that he had made to facilitate the transport of the heavy timber required for his building operations, which is floated down from the forests of Tōrwāl. I was glad to find that spiritual obligations and political cares had in no way dimmed his keen practical perception of the great economic value of the magnificent forests of Upper Swāt and of the need for their systematic protection.

For two more days my camp had to remain at Saidu—not on account of the comfortable conditions that we there enjoyed, thanks to the hospitable attention of the Bādshāh and his advisers, but because of the many ruins to be visited in the neighbouring valleys. So it was only before our start in the early morning and on our return in the evening from long excursions that I was able to catch glimpses of my host and of the daily life surrounding him. The Miāngul—to use the familiar designation inherited from his father and still the only one by which he was at that time known to the Indian Foreign Department—is a person of remarkably active habits. The month of Ramazān had then just begun. Being strictly observed here as a fast from the first sign of dawn to nightfall, it left the Faithful but little time for rest and sleep. Yet early as I started in the morning, I always found my host about, taking the fresh air on the terrace before his Darbār rooms or attending to various business.

Miāngul 'Abdul Wahāb Gul-shāhzāda Sāhib (Fig. 36) is a strongly built person of middle height, with a fine head and

36. MIĀNGUL 'ABDUL WAHĀB GUL-SHĀHZĀDA SĀHIB, RULER OF SWĀT.

strikingly intelligent and pleasant features. His age is believed to be about forty-five, but owing to the plentiful grey hairs in his flowing beard he might well be taken to be somewhat older. Like almost all Swātīs he is spare in figure, and his great fondness for 'Shikār', or game pursued on the rugged rocky hills of his country, necessarily keeps him 'lean', to use the expression that I often heard Indian students apply to friends of old Lahore days who refused to grow fat. His quickness of eye and limb impressed me as befitting the role he has to play on his newly founded throne.

That he is quick at the 'up-take', too, I learnt from our conversations; for he talks practically nothing but Pashtu, and my command of this by no means easy tongue is still defective enough to puzzle, as a rule, any new interlocutor at first. However, with the Bādshāh no such trouble marred simple conversation. Like many strong rulers in these parts he is accustomed to dispose of affairs by word of mouth and is apparently little hampered by the fact that his knowledge of Persian would scarcely allow him to scrutinize closely the actual wording of such documents as have to be issued in his name.

Yet the amount of business that he has to transact as supreme arbiter of disputes, as lord of the manor of widely scattered landed property, and as chief organizer of his revenues and armed forces, must be great; all are tasks that demand a record of some sort besides that of a reliable memory. The amount of this work could be inferred merely from the crowds of Jirgahs (tribal councils), local Khāns, and other individual applicants whom I saw early in the morning already gathered in front of the Miāngul's terrace. It seemed a very convenient substitute for that *takht* or raised seat of judgement which Indian as well as Central-Asian tradition necessarily associates with the function of a ruler.

It was curious, when returning in the evening, to meet the same miscellaneous host of Khāns, with their followers in carefully separated groups, and of humbler folk, walking slowly on the wide road that the Miāngul has made between his seat and Mingaora. They had sought relaxation from the long waits and pleadings in watching the game of football played by the schoolboys in a field laid out half-way to Mingaora. Now they were returning in the hope that the Miāngul's flesh-pots would soon enable them to break the day's fast. It is a rule enforced by tradition and policy that all those who seek justice from him must be entertained as his guests, if need be, for three days—and not more. A wise practice it seems, as calculated both to expedite judgement and to soften the feelings of disappointed litigants. Anyhow, the fiscal expense involved by this system of hospitality to litigants was obviously in the Miāngul's mind when, on my request to be allowed to pay for all supplies furnished to my party, he smilingly referred to the insignificance of the charge compared with that of the hundred or two of 'guests' whom his kitchen had to entertain daily. I was told by others of the reasonable arrangement that divides these 'guests' into three distinct classes: one partaking of the ruler's own table, another having meals with the Wazīr, and a third, made up of the common herd, who are served direct from the big kitchen. I have little doubt that this third division is quite as exacting as the others in respect of quantity and not less critical as to the cooking.

Needless to say that all these parties bringing their cases before the Bādshāh walked about fully armed. The aim of even the humblest Pathān cultivator here is to possess a rifle, revolver, or pistol, and the variety of weapons met with on the road, from the latest magazine rifles and Mauser pistols to cheap Martinis, was surprising. Obviously it is a good investment to acquire an up-to-date weapon, and as

37. BĀDSHĀH MIĀNGUL GUL-SHĀHZĀDA, RULER OF SWĀT, WITH SON AND CHIEF ATTENDANTS.

Seated from left to right: Sipāh-sālār Aḥmad ʻAlī, Wazīr Hazrat ʻAlī, Bādshāh Miāngul, Ruler of Swāt, Shāhzāda Miāngul Jahānzeb. Standing: Ataullah Khān, Rāja Shāh ʻĀlam, ʻAbdul Latīf Khān.

elsewhere across the Frontier, big prices, up to a thousand rupees and more, are paid for the best small-bore magazine rifles. The necessity of understanding the sights on these has, I imagine, something to do with the knowledge of European numeral figures of which I found curious epigraphic evidence, more than once, in graffiti on boulders by the roadside. How they may puzzle an archaeologist in the distant future!

CHAPTER X

BUDDHIST REMAINS ABOUT SAIDU AND MANGLAWAR

My visits to ruined Stūpas and other ancient remains in the valleys uniting near Saidu revealed not only sites of considerable interest but also charming mountain scenery. These valleys all descend from the boldly serrated and abundantly wooded range that divides Swāt from Bunēr. The snow-covered pyramid of Mount Ilam came again and again into view, dominating these sub-alpine landscapes. I now began to understand why legends of all sorts, some manifestly of very early origin, cluster around this peak and cause it to be reverenced not merely by the few local Hindus, hardy survivals, as it were, from pre-Muhammadan times, but also by Pathāns and Gujars. During the previous generation or two tribal turbulence and oppression had caused the latter to leave Swāt for Kashmīr with their flocks and herds. I was doubly glad to learn that they are now being drawn back to the splendid grazing-grounds of Upper Swāt. It illustrates a beneficent aspect of the peace and order that these fair lands derive from the Bādshāh's new rule. Incidentally it also gives hope that the alps and forests of Kashmīr may suffer less thereafter from over-grazing by the Gujars' destructive congeners, their buffaloes, goats, and the rest.

I look back with particular pleasure to the day spent in exploring the numerous remains in the large valley that descends from the Jaosu pass towards Saidu. It holds a number of good-sized villages, all surrounded by fertile fields, mostly on terraces. Much of this rich land has either descended to the Bādshāh as church patrimony from his holy grandfather or is held by families related to him. Passing below the precipitous hill range from which the walls crowning the crest of King Girā's Castle look down into the verdant valley, I saw ruins of ancient dwellings on more than one low spur. Then above Guligrām village we found the large Stūpa of Shināse in a fair state of preservation, and repeatedly came upon rocks by the roadside bearing Buddhist relievos (Figs. 38, 39). Almost all of them represented Bodhisattvas, in the *varamudrā* or 'pose of largess'.

Pious Muhammadan hands had done their best to deface the carvings—to throw a stone at them as one passes is considered a very meritorious act. But there was enough detail left to suggest that probably most of these figures were meant to represent Avalokiteśvara, pre-eminently the dispenser of mercy and help in the northern Buddhist Pantheon. I thought of the wide popularity that this Bodhisattva has enjoyed throughout Central Asia and has retained to this day as Kuan-yin, the 'Goddess of Mercy', in the Far East. I remembered that Hsüan-tsang had since his youth vowed fervent worship to Avalokiteśvara, and had piously attributed to his divine patron's help his escape from death by thirst in the dreaded Gobi at the very outset of his great adventurous journey. So I reflected on the pleasure with which the pilgrim's eyes must have rested on these and other similar rock-carvings.

Heavy snow still covered Mount Ilam, and so my visit to it had to be postponed till my return from the Indus two months later. But we pushed up the valley as far as Miāna. From there, at an elevation of about 5,000 feet, a fine view offered up to the wooded heights that overlook the pass of Jaosu. Spring, with its first flowers, had just arrived at this height, and the blossom of the few fruit-trees round the hamlet, with the brilliant green of the young shoots of maize in the fields, made a delightful foreground. An important route to Bunēr crosses the pass. I was therefore not surprised to find that the Bādshāh's strategic foresight had caused a good bridle-road to be made to the pass and had protected it by a fort built above the Gujar hamlet of Miāna and by towers beyond. There might more than once have been heavy fighting in this part of the valley. But local tradition prefers to ascribe the many crumbling graves that we passed in a large sombre grove of wild olive and ilex trees to young 'children of the Faith' whom 'white unbelievers' had wickedly murdered in the old times.

There were numerous Buddhist ruins also in the Janbil valley through which the route from the Khalēl pass leads down to Mingaora. There we found nearly a dozen ruinous Stūpas scattered in little groups; all had suffered badly because their accessible position had made them convenient quarries of building-stone (Figs. 40, 43). It was probable, too, that iconoclastic zeal would assert itself with special vigour in a populous neighbourhood.

By March 27th I was free to take my leave of the Bādshāh, whose kind consideration for my plans and needs had allowed me to use these bright days at Saidu to the full, and started on the explorations up the main valley to which I had so eagerly looked forward. I was bidden a very cordial farewell by the ruler in front of the platform where he dispenses justice to his people. I could read in his keen eyes appreciation of the very genuine gratitude I endeavoured to express for the generous way in which he had thrown open the whole of his dominion to me. Hazrat 'Alī Khān, the Wazīr, insisted on accompanying me with a large following to the very last houses of Saidu. But even after this, our own array had quite an imposing medieval appearance; for from here onwards Sipāh-sālār Aḥmad 'Alī everywhere escorted me, and his selected bodyguard of some thirty well-armed and well-set-up 'orderlies' (Fig. 45) greatly swelled my usual escort of local men-at-arms.

The first march was not to be a long one. It was to take me to Manglawar, a large place situated at the mouth of a

38. ROCK-CARVED RELIEVOS OF BUDDHIST DIVINITIES, BELOW SHERĀRAI.

39. ROCK-CARVED IMAGES OF BODHISATTVAS, NEAR KUKRAI.

side valley to the north of the Shamēlai spur, where the course of the Swāt river makes its sharp turn to the north. For a great portion of the year the easier route along the main valley is completely closed by the rise of the river, which washes the foot of the spur. At such times the track leads by the narrow Shamēlai pass across the rugged rocky heights of the spur. But the spring flood from the melting snows in the high mountains had been somewhat retarded by the cloudy weather that preceded my arrival at Uḍegrām, and the winter route was held to be still practicable. So we moved down through the Bāzār of Mingaora, as crowded as before, and a mile beyond reached the point on the river bank where precipitous cliffs render the track along their foot quite impracticable for animals, even unladen, at any time of the year.

Accordingly, we mounted men had to take to the wide bed of the river. Fording its several branches was not altogether a comfortable affair; for we had left Saidu after midday and the volume of water had risen greatly since the morning, the swirl of the current being strong enough to take men off their feet. Our escort, therefore, wisely kept to the footpath along the face of the cliffs. When we had safely recrossed a mile or so higher up and joined them where the sheer walls of rock recede somewhat from the river-bed, I could see how difficult that path is even for local foot traffic; for in numerous places it leads over narrow rock ledges and gimcrack wooden galleries, not unworthy to be compared to those 'Rafaks' which I remembered so well in the gorges of Hunza and the uppermost Oxus valley. I could well understand the eagerness with which the people of Upper Swāt now look forward to the time when the Bādshāh shall have carried his high road along these forbidding cliffs. It will mean, no doubt, a very tough and costly piece of engineering; but for some twenty-six miles farther up the valley the extension of the motor road would be easy enough and the gain to trade and traffic great.

Beyond this point we crossed several steep rocky knolls by the river where horses had to be led, and at one of them I was able to trace the position of an ancient *chiusa* that once guarded the passage. Thereafter, the route lay quite open across a fertile alluvial plain to Manglawar. This populous village lies at the wide mouth of an important side valley which descends from the watershed range towards the Indus. It is supposed by local tradition to have been at one time the chief place of Upper Swāt. In view of its position and its name, obviously derived from an earlier Sanskrit form *Mangala-pura*, 'the town of bliss', we can scarcely doubt the identity of Manglawar with one of the principal towns of Swāt in the seventh century A.D., which Hsüan-tsang calls Mêng-chieh-li, and Wu-k'ung Mang-o-p'o. Reports of ancient remains in the vicinity already supported this location, and examination of these ruins called for a stay of several days there.

On arrival I found that my protector, the Commander-in-chief, whether from a special sense of his responsibility for my safety or from due regard for his personal convenience, had had our camp pitched in the centre of the large village, on the terraced court in front of the house belonging to its principal landowner, Naushirwān Khān. The fact that this stands just above the lively little stream that descends from the south and divides the village did not contribute to its privacy. At first I did not much relish the cramped space, the noise made by the large company of cheery men-at-arms and the crowd outside, and other disadvantages of the site. But when heavy rain started that night and poured all through the next day, soaking everything outside my little tent and turning the ground into a pool of mud, I felt grateful enough for the shelter afforded to my people and for the convenient dark-room which 'Abdul Ghafūr, my excellent handy-man, had managed to improvise in the Khān's 'best room' and armoury combined. Advancing 'civilization' had brought here even something like a table and two iron chairs, all most welcome aids to my work.

During the next two days and part of the third the examination of ancient remains round Manglawar kept me busy. Though less numerous and extensive than those to be found in the vicinity of Bīr-kōṭ, Uḍe-grām, and Mingaora, they afforded abundant proof that Buddhist devotion once prevailed here. About half a mile to the east of the northern end of the village rises a conical hillock, undoubtedly artificial, over sixty feet above the level of the surrounding fields. It evidently represents all that survives of that great Stūpa which Hsüan-tsang describes in a corresponding position as marking the sacred spot where the Buddha in a previous birth had cut off some of his limbs as a gift of charity. The facing slabs of the Stūpa and also a good deal of the interior masonry had in the course of centuries been carried off to serve as building material in the village, as local information acknowledged and actual examination readily showed. At the foot of the hillock I thought I could just trace what seemed like the outlines of the lowest base of the Stūpa, well over two hundred feet square. Ruinous walls of ancient dwellings covered a small spur of the hill-side to the north, up to some three hundred feet above the river that descends in the valley. These structures, built on small terraces, no doubt provided shelter in troubled times for inhabitants of the town below.

Of all the Buddhist relievos found on the rocks near Manglawar and miles up the valley (Fig. 46) the colossal image of a seated Buddha some thirteen feet in height is certainly the most striking. It is carved on the vertical face of a high reddish rock, high above the narrow terrace at its foot, and is a well-executed piece of work. This position, while it had saved the relievo from damage by pious vandals, has at the same time made it distinctly difficult to photograph. The hands of the true believers must often have itched as they saw this benign-faced heathen idol looking down towards Manglawar from its height of some three hundred feet above Shakhōrai hamlet.

About a mile farther up the valley, but at a lower level on the hill-side, there were three Sanskrit inscriptions to be visited, excellently incised on huge boulders. Two of them are found at a romantic spot where on a precipitous slope a big detached rock overhangs a small spring in a grotto full of ferns and maidenhair. This cool shady retreat offered a delightful contrast to the rugged slopes above and below, where every step entangled the explorer in thickets of thorny scrub.

My attempts to make paper squeezes of these two inscriptions were unsuccessful owing to the difficult position of the engraved rock surfaces, the strong wind, and lack of time. But I managed to secure photographs of them (Fig. 41) and also of the third inscription, found a few hundred yards off on a huge granite boulder known as Khazānagat, the 'rock of the treasure'. I did not, like my escort, expect that the inscriptions, engraved in Brāhmī characters of the first or second century A.D., would reveal to us the hiding-places of great treasures. But it was rather a disappointment to find after my return from Swāt that they were identical with those which Professor George Bühler, that great departed Indologist, had published nearly thirty years before from estampages secured by Colonel Deane through a clever native agent.

What is more regrettable, however, is that these beautifully engraved and excellently preserved epigraphic records

40. RUINED MOUNDS MARKING BUDDHIST STŪPAS, SHERĀRAI.

41. BUDDHIST INSCRIPTION ON ROCK ABOVE SHAKHŌRAI.

yield no historical or antiquarian information. They merely reproduce certain famous sayings of the Buddha and brief well-known expositions of his doctrine regarding the path that leads to salvation, or rather to liberation from the cycle of mundane existences. But, no doubt, spiritual merit had been gained by the pious donors who had the inscriptions engraved, and by those whom they served to guide in the right path.

I am afraid that 'Abdul Hanān, the Pathān agent who had successfully obtained the estampages for Colonel Deane, was not one of the latter; for unable to meet his employer's demand for more 'ancient writings' of this sort, he proceeded, like that clever rogue, Islām Ākhun, whom some years later I unmasked at Khotan, to forge them. The inscribed stones that he supplied for a couple of years all showed, of course, 'unknown scripts'; for the various 'hands' that he employed among local Muhammadan theological students to make the rude engravings could scarcely be expected to learn to imitate the writing of those old Hindu infidels. Nevertheless these 'inscriptions' were duly reproduced in learned societies' journals. They might have continued to puzzle Orientalist scholars had not the forger, emboldened by success, found it more convenient later on to supply, instead of engraved stones, impressions that he pretended to have taken from inscribed rocks. The fact that the supposed originals had in reality been carved on wooden planks led in the end to the exposure of the fraud; for the impressions were found to reveal not merely the mysterious 'unknown characters' but also, only too faithfully, the natural markings of the wood on which they had been carved.

Neither at Manglawar nor elsewhere in Swāt were there many signs of that charitable regard for the life of animate beings which Buddhist doctrine has always and in all lands enjoined. We were all the more struck by a curious local custom that we here observed. About half a mile to the east of the village, alongside of the track leading up the valley, there are some large trees where wild-duck abound by day and night. They gather there in great numbers from their feeding-grounds on the network of channels and pools formed by the Swāt river and the large stream that joins it from the side of Manglawar. The birds while in the trees or flying to and from them are considered sacrosanct, though elsewhere the Swātīs eagerly shoot and trap them. No explanation was forthcoming of the asylum thus granted. Could it possibly be connected with the fact that the mound of the great ruined Stūpa already mentioned rises not far off?

CHAPTER XI

ON THE WAY TO THE SWĀT KOHISTĀN

ON the 31st March I moved my camp to Chārbāgh, a large town-like village situated about three miles farther north in the main Swāt valley and the centre of much trade. By the advantages of its position, in the midst of a wide and fertile alluvial plain, Chārbāgh might well figure among the four or five places which at one time or another are believed to have ranked as the political centre of old Swāt. A quantity of Indo-Greek and Indo-Scythian coins brought for sale was evidence that the place had long been occupied. Ruined Stūpas and debris-covered sites of ancient dwellings could also be traced at different points of the valley leading towards the Kōtkai pass, which affords easy access to Ghōrband and the Indus.

One of the ruined Stūpas rises on the flat bed of the valley about a mile to the east. It has no recognizable base and now consists merely of a bare core of masonry (Fig. 42). I thought I could identify it with Hsüan-tsang's miraculous 'Stone Stūpa'. This was situated about six miles to the north-east of Mêng-chieh-li or Manglawar, and was believed to have suddenly emerged from the ground where the Buddha had stopped to preach the Law. Here, and indeed wherever a route connects Swāt with the Miāngul's newly annexed territory to the south and east, a well-constructed new road, fit for laden transport of all kinds, attests the ruler's grasp of the strategic importance of good communications. But the *corvée* for all this must be heavy.

As I looked up towards the easy Ghōrband pass and the wide open valley leading down to Chārbāgh I thought of the relief and delight with which the old Chinese pilgrims, after travelling from Darēl through the difficult gorges of the Indus, must have greeted this view, which marked the end of their troubles. Pious Fa-hsien, who made his way down the Indus to Swāt about A.D. 403, has left us a graphic description of this terrifying 'route of the hanging chains' with all its dangers and fatigues. The formidable obstacles with which nature has beset it have also been recorded in the sober pages of the Chinese Imperial Annals. No European has ever passed these forbidding gorges of the Indus Kohistān. But I was able to hear details about its 'Rafaks' and risks direct from Rāja Shāh 'Ālam. Splendid cragsman as he is and as nimble with hands and feet as any of his Khushwakt race, he spoke with undisguised aversion of his seven days' exhausting journey down that succession of precipices overhanging the great swirling river in its narrow channel. I wish that I might yet accomplish it with him! But there is little chance of the Pax Britannica opening a way in the near future through these lawless Kohistānī communities.

Shāh 'Ālam, together with Rāja Pakhtūn Wālī's two young sons Firāmorz Khān and Jahāngīr, is now eating the bread of an exile from the Miāngul's bounty. He does it with innate dignity and with firm hope of a return of Fortune's favour. For both of these he claims my genuine regard, and, I feel, he appreciates it. Since the downfall of his uncle and master, he has twice made an attempt to regain Tangīr and Darēl, in the name of his cousins, but in each case it failed after some fighting through want of outside support. Whether it could be renewed with some chance of success, I could not judge. He had first found refuge in the mountain tracts of Kandia, which he knows well and has friends in. So I guessed that the support he now receives in Swāt may be due to reasons not altogether altruistic. History in Kashmīr and elsewhere records many examples of exiled pretenders successfully asserting their claims with the help of neighbours. So that there would

42. RUINED STŪPA STRIPPED OF ITS MASONRY FACING, NEAR CHĀRBĀGH.

43. REMAINS OF RUINED STŪPA AT JURJURAI, JANBIL VALLEY.

be nothing new in such an event. I was glad that chance had brought me into personal contact with the men who seem likely to participate in it.

From Chārbāgh I started on April 2nd on my journey up the head-waters of the Swāt river, which was to carry me as far as the present border of the Bādshāh's dominions. Beyond it lie Kalām and other alpine tracts of the Swāt Kohistān, which, though still independent, may soon become a bone of contention between him and the rulers of Dīr and Chitrāl. Of course, I had promised to take care not to prejudice future developments by going beyond the territory actually held by my host. The people of the Swāt Kohistān are of the same Dard race that inhabited the whole of Swāt down to the Pathān invasion, and I knew that it would be useful to collect specimens of the two Dardic tongues still spoken up there, together with anthropological data. Another reason that made me eager to push up the river as far as I could without giving rise to complications of a 'political' nature was that the country ahead had never been surveyed. So there was plenty of work awaiting Tōrabāz Khān, my hardy Afrīdī Surveyor, who was proving an untiring climber and a very skilful plane-tabler. I had reason, therefore, to hope that the Survey, too, would be pleased with the results of this northward extension of our tour.

An easy march past numerous fair-sized villages up the amply irrigated main valley brought us to Khwāja-khēl, a large place where a considerable stream from the watershed range towards the Indus debouches. Heavy rain started in the evening and continuing practically without a break forced us to halt there the next day. This delay was not altogether unwelcome to myself; for what with the long days spent on our hunt for ruins and 'idols', the late hours devoted to detailed diary records, work on photographic negatives, &c., it had been difficult to spare enough time for other duties—or for rest either. But I felt sorry for those who were looking after us under such weather conditions. With the exception of a few watchful sentries I found them all huddled up sound asleep in their tents, even well past midday.

The heavy downpour that had kept me all day writing in my little tent and had surrounded it with pools—they marked the sunk-in tombs of an old graveyard—fortunately ceased on April 4th and allowed a fresh move up the valley. For the first two marches the journey brought no marked change in the scenery. Though the hills on either side increased in height and approached much closer to the river, they left enough room by its banks for rice cultivation on wide terraces. Up to Churrai, which we reached on the second day, the abundance of water, coupled with adequate summer warmth, allows two crops to be raised in the year. The first is always wheat, oats, rape-seed, or a sort of lucerne, not unlike the familiar *bidar* of Turkestān. So the eye could feast on delightful stretches of fresh green, and spring flowers abounded along the low hedges bordering the fields.

The cultivated belt of alluvium is much narrower on the right or western bank, and it was this bank that I followed in order to visit the ancient remains of which reports had reached me. Each of these visits meant a stiff scramble up the hill-side, where thorny scrub invariably covered all ground that is not converted into small terraced fields. The ruins of Stūpas and monasteries which I here traced were modest in size, yet very welcome. They definitely disproved the prevailing belief that Buddhist remains do not extend beyond Chārbāgh near the big bend of the river. At the same time they afforded me reassuring evidence of the genuine endeavour of my protectors to secure whatever local information could be got about 'old things'.

44. CROWD OF STUDENTS AND OTHERS AT GARAI MADRASAH, CHAKĒSAR.
See below, page 161.

45. JAMADĀR AND MEN-AT-ARMS OF ESCORT, FROM NIKPI-KHĒL TRACT.

Without their constant help, indeed, it would have been quite impossible to trace such ruins, so little was there to distinguish the crumbling walls or mounds at a distance from the rocks or scrub of the hill-sides. It was still too early in the year for fresh grass to appear on the slopes and set off the reddish-brown remnants of walls and the heaps of potsherds usually found near them. Certain types of incised decorative motifs, simple but of good taste, are always frequent among the ceramic debris of Buddhist times, and approximate dating has thus become easy. Small money rewards for ornamented pieces soon turned my agile escort into eager hunters for such 'rubbish'.

At Sambat the tossing river had still to be crossed on a skin raft. But below Paitai, where we had to regain the left bank for the night's camp, the river-bed had narrowed sufficiently to be spanned between high rocky banks by a timber bridge. It was as yet under construction, and though planned on sound cantilever principles, the three big rafters used for its central portion swayed enough to frighten 'Mōti', the Sipāh-sālār's intelligent spaniel. He absolutely refused to cross on his own feet and had in the end to be carried over. The dog had been bought at the Mardān cantonment and his parents had obviously been accustomed to live with 'Sāhibs'. So 'Mōti' and I soon became special friends. Of course, I talked to him in English, and my Pathāns seemed to find his apparent comprehension of that 'Wilāyatī' tongue quite natural.

At Paitai an open alluvial fan, at present uncultivated, near the Bādshāh's newly built fort made a delightful camping-place. The faint scent of young thyme was in the air and somehow carried me back to far-off 'Dashts' on the uppermost Oxus or on the glacis of the K'un-lun. The next day brought much satisfaction to the antiquarian. Once again I had to carry on my archaeological search on the right bank, while the baggage, including the impedimenta of my hosts and protectors, kept to the more open ground on the eastern side of the valley.

Fully twenty-eight years have passed since I received from Colonel Deane, then Political Agent on the Malakand, the ink impression of an inscribed stone brought to him by his above-mentioned native agent, then not yet turned into a forger of such things. It showed two big footprints marked with the Buddha's emblem, the wheel of universal sovereignty, and below them a line of bold Kharoshṭhī characters. I sent the impression on at once to Professor Bühler, the greatest of Indian epigraphists and Indologists of his time. In my accompanying note I expressed the belief that the inscribed stone, said to be situated at Tirāt, a village of Upper Swāt, was probably the same that Fa-hsien and Hsüan-tsang describe as showing the miraculous footprints of the Buddha. Professor Bühler, in the brief notice he promptly published of the inscription, a couple of months before he lost his life on the Lake of Constance, showed that I was right in this conjecture; for the legend as deciphered by him distinctly describes those footprints as left by the Enlightened One when he rested at that spot.

But even before I could visit Tirāt and the sacred relic still surviving near it, my antiquarian heart was to be gratified by another discovery. Both those old Chinese pilgrims mention another sanctified spot some distance south of the stone with the footprints. It was a big rock by the river bank, on which pious eyes could still see the imprint left by the clothes which the Buddha had washed and then dried there. My local informants had told me of a 'big stone with writing' to be seen on the way to Tirāt village on the right bank of the river, and naturally my thoughts had turned at once to this second notice of my patron saint. So my satisfaction was great when on descending from

46. ROCK-CARVED RELIEVO OF BODHISATTVA, ON SLOPE OF NANGRIĀL RIDGE, ABOVE MANGLAWAR.

47. STONE WITH THE BUDDHA'S MIRACULOUS FOOTPRINTS AND KHAROSHṬHĪ INSCRIPTION, ABOVE TIRĀT.

some ruins of a small Buddhist shrine high up in the Ragast Nullah I was taken to the spot indicated.

There by the roadside rose a large mound marking a completely demolished Stūpa, and some hundred yards off above the deep-cut rocky bed of the river I was shown a huge boulder, some thirty feet long and twelve feet high (Fig. 48), covered on its fairly smooth southern side with numerous graffiti in Sanskrit and also in Arabic characters. The former were so weathered and effaced that I was unable to decipher more than a few auspicious syllables; but these sufficed to show that these scribblings went back to early medieval times, when Buddhism in its Hinduized form still prevailed in these parts. The Arabic graffiti, most of them repeating the Islamic creed or Kalimah, also had their interest, as attesting continuity of local worship. But of the holy markings left by the Buddha's garments no trace remained—except the place which they had once occupied. Over a space fully eleven feet high and eight feet wide the smooth surface had been completely scraped off. Was this the handiwork of some fervent Mullahs, propagandists of Islām, which is known to have penetrated into the Swāt Kohistān only some eight or ten generations ago,—or of relic-hunting devotees of old?

Curiously enough, local worship had here derived fresh nourishment from a recent event. Between the Stūpa mound and the road I found a grave mound marked by votive offerings of various kinds. It held the remains of an unfortunate Afrīdī who some two or three years before had come as a trader of rifles, a very valued commodity in these parts, and had been murdered not far off by some men from the Kohistān. His grave was appropriately placed here and is now receiving due worship as the resting-place of a Shahīd or martyr. If life is of little account as yet in this region, there is anyhow some compensation to be found in the ease with which a violent death converts the sinful victim into a martyr.

A stiff climb over thickly wooded slopes, where I met the first cedars intermingled with firs and wild olives, took me from the 'clothes-washing' site up the picturesque side valley that holds the scattered hamlets of Tirāt. There on a terraced field, facing the largest of them across a deep-cut stream, I was duly shown the inscription, engraved on the smooth face of a big fragment of rock. Turned sideways and half-hidden in the ground, it now serves as part of a stone fence by the side of a narrow lane (Fig. 47). The two footprints, though engraved only to a slight depth, might well seem impressive, being fully nineteen inches in length. But how 'the size varied with the religious merit of the measurer', as Hsüan-tsang's 'Memoirs' tell us, it would be difficult now to guess.

The shape of the stone left no doubt that it was placed originally with its flat surface upwards. It had evidently been thrown out when the shrine which held it was destroyed. Luckily the owners of the adjoining fields, though Mullahs and hence men of religion, had seen nothing in the stone to offend their orthodox feelings or to mislead their flock. Otherwise the stone might well have been defaced or conveniently reburied when it was accidentally brought to light again many years ago. The impression sent to Bühler in 1897 was a good one. So I could content myself with using the remaining daylight to take photographs and rapidly survey two ruined mounds close by. One of them, some forty feet across its flat top and of unusual shape, doubtless hides the remains of the shrine that our saintly Chinese guide mentions as having been erected over the miraculous footprints.

48. BOULDER MARKING SPOT OF 'BUDDHA'S CLOTHES-WASHING', ON RIGHT BANK OF SWĀT RIVER.

49. MOSQUE AND CROWD AT CHURRAI, TŌRWĀL.

CHAPTER XII

THE ENTRY INTO TŌRWĀL

As the night fell we made our way from Tirāt down to the river, some eight hundred feet below, and crossing once again to the left bank reached the large village of Churrai. It is the gate to the Swāt Kohistān or Tōrwāl, the name given to the portion of the Swāt valley absorbed four years before in the Bādshāh's dominion. Churrai, with its closely packed dwellings and lanes scarcely wide enough for two ponies to pass, is quite a busy place of local trade. From there come all the closely woven and gaily but tastefully coloured woollen blankets that India knows as 'Swātī rugs'. They are made by the womenfolk in the side valley of Chihil-dara, which descends to Churrai from the high snowy peaks towards Kāna and Dubēr on the east, and to some extent also in other smaller valleys of Tōrwāl.

That this local industry of Tōrwāl is as ancient as the Dard race that retains its hold there is proved by a passage which M. Sylvain Lévi, the eminent French Indologist, has quoted in his comments on a curious Buddhist Sanskrit text published by him under the title of *La géographie des Yakshas*. It contains lists of demons whom pious legend associated as a kind of *genii loci* with particular localities in different parts of India and especially in its Frontier region. In that passage which by its Chinese translations is shown to belong to the early centuries of our era, we already find the rugs of Uḍḍiyana or Swāt mentioned by the same term of *kambala* that is now applied in Indian vernaculars to these textile products of Tōrwāl. Indian literature, so strikingly deficient, alas, in records of real history or geography, can scarcely contain any earlier testimony to the antiquity of a still flourishing local industry.

Unfortunately, though the ancient skill in weaving and

the use of traditional patterns still survive, the introduction of aniline dyes has here, as elsewhere in the East, brought about a sad and rapid decline in the harmonious blending of colours. Rugs produced with the fine old vegetable dyes, such as were still obtainable at Peshawar some thirty years ago, could now no longer be found for me even in the remote tract where this manufacture has had its home for so many centuries.

At Churrai the chance of collecting my first specimens of Tōrwālī, a Dard language so far practically unrecorded, and of taking anthropological measurements among its speakers, detained me for a day (Fig. 49). This occupation was pleasantly varied by a walk through the narrow lanes, where many doors and shop recesses showed excellent wood-carving (Fig. 50), and along the lively stream which comes down from the side valley of Chihil-dara. Upper Swāt abounds in life-giving water, and now that the melting snows were filling all these mountain torrents it was a constant feast for the eyes to watch their tossing white cascades.

The sound of the rushing water and of the rapids of the young Swāt river was loud enough. But it was by no means sufficient to drown the local noises at night-time. They came not only from the wide-awake cocks and babies of the village in the immediate vicinity of which we had been forced to camp for want of other space. A considerable proportion was contributed by my protective force, some forty men in all, as a result of the Ramazān fast. What with the evening meal put off until nightfall and the necessity of taking the only other meal permitted by sacred law long before the first dawn, the men seemed to think it scarcely worth while to take any sound sleep between. Preparations for cooking the early meal usually began about midnight, and there were always little groups chattering while they eagerly watched the process. How, with so little regular sleep, the

50. WOOD-CARVINGS ON DOOR OF HOUSE, CHURRAI.

51. BRIDGE OVER SWĀT RIVER AT AĪN, BELOW BRANIĀL.

men were able to keep up a brisk walk on the day's march was a marvel. There is plenty of lively resilience in Pathān physique and mentality, and the capacity for taking sleep in snatches at any time probably proves useful not only to great men like Napoleon but to humbler mortals also.

From Churrai onwards the valley rapidly contracted and the scenery soon began to recall that of the Jhelam valley below Kashmīr (Fig. 51). Glorious weather favoured the first march, which brought us past picturesque hamlets high up on wooded spurs to Braniāl, the chief place of the Tōrwālī-speaking hillmen (Fig. 52). But there our luck changed. Two days of rain, at times quite torrential, kept us at Braniāl in conditions not altogether enjoyable. The narrow terrace outside the newly built fort where our camp had of necessity been placed was soon thoroughly soaked, and for even a few steps outside my little tent I needed the stout mountain boots that I had brought from Oxford.

Fortunately I was able to employ this long halt to good purpose, overtaking the formidable arrears of correspondence with which my constant moves were threatening to submerge me, and recording specimens of Tōrwālī stories for publication by my friend Sir George Grierson, in connexion with his monumental *Linguistic Survey of India*. I am no expert in Dard philology and not endowed with a very keen ear. So it was doubly fortunate that the Braniāl reciter whom Rāja Shāh 'Ālam secured for me was, like most of his fellow Tōrwālīs, a person rather slow of tongue and brain, and the composition of his tales accordingly simple. The constant repetition of phrases but slightly varied served me well in a quasi-Ollendorfian fashion, and in the end the word-for-word translation of the record taken did not prove so difficult a task as I had at first feared it would be on account of my imperfect command of Pashtu. It was through this medium that all our conversation had to be carried on, and neither Mukadir Shāh, the Tōrwālī, nor Shāh 'Ālam, the Khushwakt from Yāsīn and Tangīr, nor myself had a thorough mastery of Pashtu.

But Shāh 'Ālam combines with other excellent qualities a real linguistic ability, and Chitrālī, Shinā, Kohistānī, all of which he fluently speaks in addition to Persian, Pashtu, and a little Hindustānī, are, as Dard languages, allied to Tōrwālī. The latter, like the other dialects of old Dard stock spoken by independent tribes in the Indus gorges, is bound to be swept away in course of time by the ever advancing tide of Pathān speech. So I felt some gratification at this opportunity of adding to the extremely scanty knowledge so far available of this linguistic 'relict'. The total population of Tōrwāl can scarcely exceed six thousand souls. Significantly enough it includes quite a number of immigrant families speaking Chitrālī or Pashtu. And in addition to all this mixture, there are numerous Gujars, familiar to me from residence in Kashmīr, grazing their cattle high up in the side valleys and cultivating on lease such little plots as Tōrwālīs can spare them.

But my halt at Braniāl enabled me to make interesting observations also in another direction. When I visited the village on the day of my arrival I was greatly struck by the amount of fine wood-carving, old and new, to be seen in this quaint rabbit-warren of houses (Fig. 55). The lanes between them are incredibly crooked and narrow. But a curious method of 'town planning' secures unexpected open spaces owing to the fact that the flat roofs of certain groups of these houses, most of them of two stories, are combined into little piazzas. These roofs are made accessible to fellow citizens or strangers by primitive stairs or ladders. The houses are built mainly of timber with wattled walls, and recalled those of the early centuries after Christ which I had excavated from the sands of the Tak-

52. GROUP OF TŌRWĀLĪS AT BRANIĀL.

53. WOODEN PILLARS WITH CARVINGS IN LOGGIA OF PRINCIPAL MOSQUE, BRANIĀL.

lamakān at the Niya Site and elsewhere. My general impression was that the methods of building and living in this mountain tract, difficult of access and so little exposed to outside influences, cannot have changed greatly since the times when Lower Swāt with its fertile lands enjoyed its flourishing civilization of Buddhist times, or when, even earlier, Bactrian-Greek chiefs, bringing Hellenistic traditions in speech and material culture, held sway there.

This earlier phase in the history of the North-West Frontier was vividly called up before my eyes by the remarkable variety of decorative motifs of purely Graeco-Buddhist art displayed in the abundant wood-carving on the doors, pillared verandahs, &c., of Braniāl houses (Figs. 53, 54). This is not the place to discuss details. It must suffice to state briefly that many of the most frequent designs, floral scrolls (often including the acanthus), bands of ornamental diapers, &c., with which I was so familiar in the Gandhāra relievos, as well in wood-carvings at ancient sand-buried sites in the Tārīm basin, have survived practically intact in this far-off corner of the mountains. Distinct traces of the influence once exercised by Graeco-Buddhist art in the Indus region had previously forced themselves upon my atte[illegible]n in Chitrāl, Darēl, and elsewhere in the Hindukush region. But nowhere was evidence of it so striking as in this surviving craft of the Tōrwāl wood-carvers. I did my best to secure specimens of it for our New Delhi Museum of the future in the shape of old carved brackets and panels thrown away as useless lumber, and also had rough drawings made by a local craftsman.

CHAPTER XIII

TO THE HEADWATERS OF THE SWĀT RIVER

On the 11th April I was able to set out again up the valley in order to reach the extreme northern limit of the Bādshāh's dominion. From Braniāl onwards the hardy Swāt mules had to be replaced by human transport (Fig. 64). The ruler had lost no time after his annexation of Tōrwāl in getting a road made practicable for ponies and mules. But it would not have been safe to use it for laden transport after the damage caused by the recent heavy rain and, in some places, by avalanches. The two marches that carried me to Pēshmāl, the Bādshāh's last village on the Swāt river, led through scenery of quite an alpine character. The route led up and down along steep spurs and across picturesque side valleys flanked by mountains still snow-covered (Fig. 56). No archaeological remains were to be looked for in such surroundings. But it was delightful to feel that I was moving between mountains on which no European eye had hitherto rested, at least not since classical times. To the east, where the high watershed range divides the Swāt river drainage from the Indus, snowy crests and peaks, like walls of crystal—as the old Chinese pilgrim Sung Yün put it—gleamed at the head of each narrow side valley (Fig. 57).

All the higher slopes were clothed with magnificent conifer forest up to 9,000–10,000 feet, and from Ramēt onwards, about half-way up on the first march, deodars and then firs and pines of magnificent stature became more and more frequent, even along the 'road'. There was, unfortunately, much evidence of the destructive methods of work of the Kāka-khēl sept of Nowshera, those saintly timber-contractors who for years had had a free hand in their dealings with the Kohistānīs of Swāt and elsewhere. Some of the

54. LOGGIA WITH WOOD-CARVINGS, YAHYA MALIK'S HOUSE, BRANIĀL.

55. LANE IN BRANIĀL, LOOKING UP VALLEY.

56. VIEW OF ASRET VALLEY FROM ABOVE RIGHT BANK OF SWĀT RIVER.

57. NORTHERN SPUR OF KOSHUJAN MASSIF, SEEN FROM OPPOSITE AIRANAI.

more accessible spurs had been badly denuded, while in places huge trees had been felled and left unsawn owing to some squabble with the Tōrwālī wood-cutters. All this destructive exploitation has happily been stopped since the ruler of Swāt established his hold on the Kohistān. He realizes the value of its timber resources and is setting about their utilization in a more intelligent fashion.

We halted for the first night at Chōdgrām, under the protection of a small timber-built fort (Fig. 58) quite antique in appearance, though new. Here a glorious view opened over the Mankiāl valley and the bold ice-crowned peaks that close it to the east. They were the same great peaks that I had first sighted far away from the Malakand, rising to heights not far from 19,000 feet. Chōdgrām itself lies on a spur high above the confined gorges of the river, and this made the vista wonderfully wide and impressive. I only wish my photographs could have done full justice to it (Fig. 59).

On the next day's march to Pēshmāl we had to keep for the most part low down by the river. But there was plenty of true alpine scenery on which to feast one's eyes, to say nothing of the lovely colours of the river water, which showed every shade of green, and of charming glimpses up the cascading streams that come down to feed it. No more villages were to be seen here, only scattered homesteads clinging to the green slopes, where water could be brought to irrigate small terraced fields. It had been pleasant to note, as we moved higher and higher up the valley, how the number of fruit-trees increased. We had been travelling in the wake of spring, and at Churrai the apricots and apple-trees were already in full bloom. But up here, at elevations of 6,000 to 7,000 feet, only little flowers in sheltered spots announced the coming of spring, and the big walnut-trees still stood as bare as they did a month ago in Kashmīr.

From Pēshmāl, a rude Gujar hamlet, I enjoyed a grand sight of the big boldly serrated snowy spur thrown out northward by the high massif above Mankiāl (Fig. 60). Glaciers of some size descend from this spur. But what delighted me even more was the vista from our high-lying camping-place towards the north. There a grand wall of snowy mountains rose before me, and I knew that it marked the approach to that distant Hindukush region which holds Mastūj and Yāsīn, full for me of happy recollections of my travels in 1906 and 1913.

Next morning, with a temperature only a little above freezing-point, I made an early start with the Sipāh-sālār and his host. We were to push ahead to the ridge of Korunduke, which marks the boundary between Tōrwāl and the still independent tribal community of Gārwī-speaking hillmen who hold the headwaters of the Swāt river. I had been promised from there a full view of Kalām, the big village situated at the meeting-place of the two main branches of the Swāt river, which come from Ushu and Utrōt. The hope was not disappointed. When the ridge was reached after a rapid climb of three miles, a glorious panorama lay before me (Fig. 61).

The reports that credited Kalām with a big expanse of open arable land were true. Nestling below an amphitheatre of mountains all still carrying snow lies a fertile little plain, which seems to mark the basin of an ancient lake scooped out probably by glacier action. To eyes that had grown accustomed to deeply eroded gorges this plain looked quite imposing. Above it, only a little over two miles from our ridge, stretched the long lines of houses, built in tiers, that form the chief place of Kalām.

It looked quite an inviting place from that distance, with dense forest coming down to it over a gentle glacis of the sheltering range. Such might some prosperous little town

58. CHŌDGRĀM VILLAGE SEEN FROM SOUTH: SNOWY RANGE ABOVE KALĀM IN DISTANCE.

59. SNOWY PEAKS ABOVE JABA VALLEY SEEN FROM ABOVE CHŌDGRĀM.

On extreme left is seen pass of Chonkur-kandao leading to Dubēr valley.

appear at the foot of the Swiss or Bavarian Alps. It was for me a strangely elevating sensation that though further progress was barred by 'political considerations', I had sighted land that seemed by comparison next door to Chitrāl, Yāsīn, and Tangīr. Once again it had fallen to my lot to approach by a new route the huge barrier of the Hindukush, that true divide between India and Central Asia.

I had brought with me Tōrabāz Khān, my indefatigable Surveyor, in order to make sure that due justice should be done to the geographical interest of the still forbidden ground before us. The big peak of Mankiāl, 18,750 feet in height and locally known as Koshujan, proved to be the only trigonometrically determined point within the fine panoramic view to the south (Fig. 62). But together with lower peaks observed on our way up it sufficed to fix our position with a fair degree of accuracy. The three hours we spent there on survey and photographic work will long be remembered by me with joy. Thin layers of snow still covered the ridge on its northern face. But wherever the sun's warm rays reached sheltered spots among the rocks pale blue violets were to be found in profusion. They had little or no scent, these dear messengers of *primavera*. Yet I greeted them with quite as great delight as those first wild cyclamens I had picked a year before on the wooded crest above the lake of Albano. Once again our globe seemed to me to become strangely small.

Reluctantly I hurried back the same day to Chōdgrām to bid *au revoir* to those glittering peaks above Mankiāl. Thence a day later we returned to Braniāl. It had to be reached in time for the due celebration of the 'Akhtar' or Īd, which marks the close of the Ramazān. A day's halt in honour of the great feast allowed me to give a good treat to my Swāt friends and the hardy escort (Fig. 63). It was a pleasure to see how quickly the big heaps of pilaw disappeared among three score of mouths which for a month had not touched food or drink in daylight. I was also able to use this halt to secure further anthropological measurements of Tōrwālīs (Fig. 52).

On April 16th the return journey down Tōrwāl was resumed. It seemed cruel to withdraw my protecting host from the flesh-pots of hospitable Braniāl; for the Īd feasting had continued long into the night, and seeing that it followed such long privations, some relaxation of spirits was inevitable. All the same a double march was accomplished to Paitai. A short half-way halt at Churrai allowed me to acquire some fair specimens of those gay-coloured 'Swātī rugs' to which I have already referred. Long before I could dispatch them as presents to distant friends, I had myself occasion to feel grateful for the warmth of these heavy woollen coverings.

60. VIEW DOWN THE SWĀT RIVER VALLEY FROM ABOVE PĒSHMĀL.

High spur of Koshujan massif seen on left.

61. PANORAMIC VIEW OF HEAD OF SWĀT RIVER VALLEY, WITH KALĀM AND MOUTHS OF UTRŌT AND USHU VALLEYS, FROM KORUNDUKE RIDGE ABOVE PĒSHMĀL.

On left Jāiban hamlet in foreground, entrance to Utrōt valley in distance. On right mouth of Ushu valley. Kalām village in centre. Tōrabāz Khān at plane-table in right bottom corner.

62. PANORAMIC VIEW OF THE SNOWY RANGE ABOVE MANKIĀL, WITH THE KOSHUJAN PEAKS (18,750 FEET) IN MIDDLE, SEEN FROM KORUNDUKE RIDGE ABOVE PĒSHMĀL.

CHAPTER XIV

ACROSS THE SWĀT-INDUS WATERSHED

I WAS now anxious to get to work east of the Swāt-Indus watershed, and therefore decided to make my way across it by the nearest pass that might be expected to be sufficiently clear of snow for laden transport. A second march led down the left bank of the river and allowed me to see more rock-carved Buddhist images (Fig. 66). Towards the end of it we turned up the big valley that debouches at Khwāja-khēl and reached the village of Shālpin below the Karōrai pass. Light showers had accompanied us during most of the morning and again later caused a hasty break-up of the roadside halt during which my Swātī protectors enjoyed their tea (Fig. 65). But after a warm and sunny afternoon I was little prepared for the heavy downpour that followed a thunderstorm late in the evening. Accompanied by violent wind, it continued all through the night. My fear that the tent would collapse through the yielding of the wooden pegs in the sodden soil was fortunately not realized. But my dismay was great when in the morning I found that a little stream of liquid mud had made its way underneath my camp-bed and had passed by the cameras. How it failed to penetrate them was a wonder to be accounted for only by the solid English leather of which their cases had been made some twenty years ago. The path above the camp had been turned into a watercourse by the torrents of rain, and when the side of it gave way had spread its muddy stream over the terrace below.

The next day, April 18th, was wretchedly wet, and all I could do in the midst of rain and deep mud was to attend to heavy arrears of writing. On the morning of April 19th the sun at last struggled through the mist and clouds that shrouded the mountains. We were only too glad to leave our sodden terrace as soon as the tents were half-dried. Once again I admired the cheerful goodwill of our escort. The Bādshāh's 'men-at-arms' clothe themselves as best they can. This means that few of them have more than a single suit of thin cotton garments, with perhaps a large sheet of the same material to sleep under. The solid leather bandoliers or more elaborate Sam Browne belts, neatly packed with cartridges, that they all display do not help to give protection from cold and damp. Fortunately Pathān villagers observe the hospitable law of their race and provide strung cots and cotton 'Razais' so far as they can. Failing these their Gujar *métayers*, characteristically called Fakīrs, *i.e.* beggars, together with all other folk cultivating but not owning land, are called on to contribute from their humble belongings. But on such nights I felt doubly uneasy for the sentries who kept constant guard over my tent and person. The only thing I could do to alleviate their lot was to lend two waterproof sheets which could be spared from my own men's equipment.

The well-graded bridle-path, one of the network of 'strategic roads' with which the Bādshāh's wise forethought has spanned his newly consolidated kingdom, made the ascent to the Karōrai pass easy for the first seven miles. Then we got into soft fresh snow and, when the top was reached at an elevation of about 6,400 feet, the ridge clothed with fine firs and pines presented as wintry an aspect as I could wish to see after a rainless 'cold weather' in Delhi. A thick white mist was clinging to both sides of the ridge, and after trudging with Tōrabāz Khān, the Surveyor, for about half a mile along its fairly level crest, we had to abandon the hope of making a 'fixing' with the plane-table. We could get only passing glimpses through rifts in the mist into the maze of deep-cut gorges draining eastwards into the Ghōrband river and thus into the Indus.

63. FEAST AFTER RAMAZĀN AT BRANIĀL.
Seated in centre: Sipāh-sālār Aḥmad 'Alī, 'Abdul Latīf Khān, and Rāja Shāh 'Ālam.

64. TŌRWĀLĪ LOAD-CARRIERS COLLECTED AT CHŌDGRĀM.

65. ROADSIDE HALT FOR TEA OF SIPĀH-SĀLĀR AND ESCORT, ABOVE KHWĀJA-KHĒL.

66. ROCK-CARVED RELIEVO OF AVALOKITEŚVARA BODHISATTVA, HALF-BURIED IN DETRITUS, NEAR JĀRE VILLAGE.

The setting-up and reading of the mercurial mountain barometer on the pass was a trying operation, for an icy wind was blowing at a temperature just about freezing-point. When this, in spite of benumbed fingers, had been safely accomplished I was glad to hurry down to where, half a mile or so beyond, the men of the escort were warming themselves round a fire at the foot of an old pine-tree. Here the two little aluminium tins containing my 'tiffin', warmed over the embers, provided welcome comfort.

A mile or so farther the snow was left behind, and the mist lifting from the slopes below revealed a landscape that looked strangely bare and stern under a grey sky after the green expanse of the open Swāt valley and the alpine charms of Tōrwāl. Only a thin growth of firs and cedars could be seen on the upper portion of the slopes, while such villages and hamlets as might be found in the deep gorges of Ghōrband were hidden from view. Our goal was the main village in the side valley of Lilaunai, which joins that of Ghōrband from the north near the sharp bend that the latter makes eastwards. At last it came suddenly into view as the path, by a narrow gap, crossed the shaly spur that we were following.

A steep descent to the confined bottom of the valley only helped to confirm that first sombre impression. Owing to the elevation, about 5,300 feet above sea-level, and still more, perhaps, owing to the high range which overlooks Lilaunai from the south and reduces the sunshine, vegetation down below still seemed very backward. The big plane-trees and elms that guard a Ziārat and burial-ground on the right bank of the considerable stream had not yet put on leaves. Otherwise it seemed the finest grove of leafy trees that we had so far seen. Swāt and adjacent tracts are singularly devoid of arbours or orchards such as the living might enjoy, a fact attributable, as we have seen, to the Pathān system of *wēsh* or periodical redistribution of lands among the families belonging to the same tribal sub-division.

But the dead fare better in this respect. Around and over their graves thickets of ilex, wild olive, and other trees, according to the nature and elevation of the ground, are allowed to grow up. Time turns righteous and wicked alike into 'Shahīds' or holy martyrs, and the sanctity thus bestowed upon burial-places protects the trees from the villagers' otherwise reckless axe. In fact, these burial-groves become sanctuaries for whatever timber, hay, &c., may be deposited there by individual villagers for future use.

What was to be seen at Lilaunai, after we had reached it by a bridge newly built by the Bādshāh's order across the tossing stream, did not help to relieve its first rather gloomy aspect. As the Sipāh-sālār, who knows all his master's conquests like his pocket and has done much to secure them, explained to me, the village had suffered to an unusual extent from internal feuds, until the Bādshāh some four years before swept into his net all these valleys between the Indus and the Swāt watershed. Ruined homesteads, roofless houses, cut fruit-trees met the eye in more than one place before we reached the Bādshāh's newly erected fort, quite medieval in structure, which now enforces peace (Fig. 67). The Pāpinī Saiyids, who hold Lilaunai, claim saintly descent; but this does not, of course, prevent them from dearly cherishing their enmities and from being much given to violence otherwise. So the Bādshāh has wisely put a capable man here, chosen from among his old supporters, to hold combined military and civil control; a true 'Vogt' as they called them in Switzerland in old times. He in turn has taken care to get a comparatively strong fort built, of course, by the Saiyids themselves.

The good quarters provided on its upper floor proved a

67. NEWLY BUILT FORT AT LILAUNAI.
Baggage being loaded in foreground.

68. PATHĀN TOMB WITH ENGRAVED HEADSTONES, BELOW BILKĀNAI.

boon to my Swātī friends and their myrmidons; for the night brought more rain, and this, with short interruptions, continued all through the following day. My dripping tent, closely surrounded by guard and kitchen tents, timber-stacks, odorous refuse-heaps among boulders, &c., was not exactly an ideal place for writing. But I was able to do a good deal of it, the roar of the torrent just below drowning all other noises. The Shilkai pass, by which I had hoped to reach the head of the Kāna valley to the north-east, had been reported still blocked by heavy snow. But the Sipāh-sālār, keen soldier that he is, with a good eye for the map that he carries in his head, realized the time that would be wasted and the opportunities for survey that would be lost if I had to change my proposed route for a detour down the Ghōrband valley. So messengers were dispatched to the Kāna Khāns for a contingent to clear a way through the snow from their side while the commandant of Lilaunai sent up gangs of Gujars and miscellaneous 'Fakīrs', that *misera contribuens plebs*, from his own.

A tramp down the rapidly narrowing gorge of the Lilaunai stream over dripping cliffs and soaked cultivation terraces, in search of a reported 'written rock', proved fruitless; for the markings borne by the big boulder were natural. But the climb that I undertook next day with the Surveyor in order to resume map-work proved more fruitful. By a three hours' steady climb a good survey station was reached on the high spur of Jabo-sar dividing the lower portions of the Lilaunai and Kāna valleys. It provided a good distant view towards three or four high snowy peaks to the north that had previously been triangulated on one of the Black Mountain expeditions across the Indus; and we were fortunately able to complete a round of theodolite bearings to unsurveyed heights south and east by the early afternoon, when the steadily gathering clouds blotted out once more all distant views.

I thought it an encouraging omen that the view to the south had allowed me to catch a short glimpse of the long thickly wooded range that stretches from the head of the Ghōrband valley due east to where the Indus makes a big bend round its foot above Thākōt. It was to that end of the range that my lamented friend Colonel Wauhope, late of the Survey of India, on the strength of the impressions he had gained at Thākōt in 1892 on the last Black Mountain expedition, had directed my attention when years before we discussed at Dehra Dun the problem of Aornos. The inquiries subsequently made on my behalf by Colonel James, then Political Agent on the Malakand, pointed to the ridge known as Pīr-sar, an eastern outlier of that range, as a likely position for the famous rock fastness that had so long been searched for. But not much reliance could be placed on the reports of native informants, naturally eager to supply the 'Mulkī Sāhib' with a suitable answer to his queries, and only by an actual survey could the question be cleared up.

CHAPTER XV

OVER THE SHILKAI PASS AND DOWN KĀNA

On my return to the Lilaunai fort I was welcomed by the report that the pass to the head of Kāna had been made practicable for load-carrying men on the morrow, provided no fresh snow fell. We all prayed that this condition might be fulfilled, and a perfectly clear morning on April 22nd brought the anxiously awaited chance. The baggage had to be divided into as small loads as practicable and distributed among the big crowd of men collected for the crossing. So it was nearly 10 a.m. before a start could be made. Under a brilliantly clear sky the narrow side valley up which the route led to the north-east looked quite bright by contrast with the gloomy aspect of the preceding three days. A couple of mosques, adorned with effective if rather crude wood-carvings on columns and brackets, had escaped the general ruin that prolonged local feuds had brought upon the valley. Spring had now at last arrived, and the lower slopes on either side, bared long ago of the conifer forest that covered all the rest of the mountains above us, had quickly responded to its call, gladdening the eyes with their first fresh green.

The snow-covered pass came into full view after five miles of easy progress, and three more brought us to its foot on a small alpine meadow. The fresh snow was just melting here; farther on it made the ascent to the pass over the grassy slopes very troublesome. The bridle-path on the opposite or southern side of the gully was completely obliterated under heavy masses of snow, and a new track had therefore to be followed. Passing clusters of load-carrying men who took rest wherever the ground under trees gave a better foothold, we at last, about 2 p.m., reached the crest by a narrow track. Men sent ahead had trodden it in the snow, which lay here four to five feet deep.

It was strange to be met towards the close of the climb by sounds of weird music, produced by drum, fife, and bagpipe. It was the little troop of the Khān of Bilkānai who had brought up the three performers, along with a large posse of carriers to relieve the Lilaunai men struggling up through the snow. The effect was distinctly encouraging, and long before I had finished my photographic work and modest 'tiffin', all the loads had changed hands and were rapidly being passed down the steep slopes towards Kāna. So eager were the Lilaunai men to get clear of their burdens and of the bitterly cold wind blowing over the crest that the headmen would scarcely wait for the special reward that I wished to have distributed among the carriers. Aneroid and hypsometer indicated a height of approximately 9,400 feet.

From a little hillock above the track, which being clear of trees was covered by heavy snowdrift, a fine but limited view was obtained to the south. It extended over most of the Indus-Swāt watershed, with Mount Ilam, that great landmark of Swāt and Bunēr, far away in the distance. But a much grander panorama opened to the north and north-east; there a continuous wall of snowy heights, with peaks from 14,000 to 15,000 feet, encircles the head of the Kāna valley, which spreads before the eyes like a huge amphitheatre (Fig. 69). Beyond that glittering white wall lay the unexplored high valley of Dubēr, belonging to the Indus Kohistān. The steep pass that gives access to it could be seen by the side of a prominent peak. The narrow avalanche-swept gully below it, as seen through my glasses, seemed impracticable at this season. Yet on our descent to Kāna we met a small band of sturdy Dubēr men who, with loads of salt and other merchandise from Swāt, were on their way to attempt it in spite of the abnormally late snowfall.

69. VIEW FROM SHILKAI PASS TOWARDS SNOWY RANGE AT HEAD OF KĀNA VALLEY.

70. RETAINERS OF KHĀNS OF KĀNA GATHERED AT DAMŌRAI.

For over two miles down from the crest progress meant a succession of jumps from one deep hole trodden in the snow into the next—or else immersion in soft snow. Then came a mile of wading in slush or small streams draining the rapidly melting fresh snow. At last dry ground was reached near the Gujar huts of Charrai, and the scramble down over trackless stony slopes, tiresome as it was, seemed a welcome change. At an elevation of about 7,000 feet we gained the bridle-path that comes down from the proper pass. It impressed me as quite a respectable piece of recent local engineering, as it winds along the cliffs that line the bottom of a narrow deep-cut valley for close on five miles.

On the steep slopes above no forest was to be seen, but cultivation terraces rose in tiers to a height of a thousand feet or so above the rock-cut channel of the stream. Here and there rib-like ridges running down from the big spurs on either side of the valley bore clusters of storied dwellings. No vegetation as yet clothed the slopes between them. In the evening light the whole valley in its monotonous hues of dark brown and deep red looked distinctly gloomy. The sharp outlines of the dwellings clinging to step-like terraces high above us, instead of relieving the gloom, only helped to produce the forbidding effect of a Doré landscape.

At some places little crowds of villagers who had descended from their heights were watching our progress below the cliffs. Evidently this visit of ours was a great and unwonted event for this far-off valley. Perhaps it also afforded some little compensation for the hard work which, evidently in view of it, had been put into repairing the Bādshāh's road at particularly difficult points below rotten rock faces. At one place we came upon a small group of well-set-up cheerful people from Dubēr in the independent Indus Kohistān. They were about to return to their valley with big loads of salt and cotton fabrics, which they had carried up from the shops of Chārbāgh. To see the respect and delight with which my Khushwakt friend was greeted by these sturdy hill-men, next-door neighbours to the great valley of Kandia where Shāh 'Ālam with the family of his murdered uncle and chief had first sought refuge after the upheaval in Tangīr, was a touching proof of the attachment still enjoyed by him as an exile from his kingdom *in spe*.

It was with a feeling of relief that below the hamlet of Larai I turned at last into the main valley of Kāna. Here at its head, below that great amphitheatre of snow-covered mountains, it proved unexpectedly wide and open. Still less was I prepared for the grand fashion in which I found our camp laid out at Bilkānai. Dōst Muhammad Khān, the son of Amīr Khān, who holds upper Kāna by a kind of feudal tenure, is acting now as 'Tahsīldār' or bailiff for the Bādshāh. In order to show due consideration for his master's chief commander and his host, he had enclosed the terraced field where our tents were pitched with lines of young pine-trees brought down from the mountains. They were hung with strings of gay paper flags in true Indian fashion.

With paths neatly laid out between the tents, the whole scene presented a striking contrast to the grim old fortified residence of the Khān, under the protection of which the camp was pitched (Fig. 71). The construction of the little stronghold was peculiar. High solid square walls, without any openings except loopholes, contained quarters built round a high square keep. Nor were there openings on the roof of the quarters, and as from regard for the Khān's household I could not proceed beyond the dark entrance-hall which serves both as stable and followers' quarters, the arrangement for lighting and airing this safe baronial retreat remained rather puzzling.

I spent a very pleasant day at Bilkānai. While the Surveyor proceeded to a high isolated hill up the valley, I examined the remains of ancient dwellings that spread some distance up the spur known on account of them as Kandarosar, and then climbed to its summit at a height of about 8,800 feet. My reward was a glorious panoramic view, including snowy passes towards Dubēr and Chihil-dara, and I found abundance of edelweiss lower down, just appearing under the influence of the first sunny spring days. The descent to some almost completely decayed ruins led by a goat track down a side of the mountain so steep and so slippery that if previous inspection had been possible I might well have felt tempted to leave them alone.

On April 24th, after recording specimens of the Dardic dialect spoken by some Dubēr men whom Shāh 'Ālam had collected, I started down the valley. The quest of Aornos was now drawing me eagerly to the south, towards the far-stretching range that divides the drainage of the Ghōrband river and its chief tributary, the river of Kāna, from the hill tract of Chakēsar. It was on the eastern extremity of this range that the long-sought-for site was most likely to be found. But for the attraction of this goal I should gladly have spared a little more time for Kāna; so bright was the scenery of this fertile open valley and so cheering the hearty welcome of its Khāns and people. Even the many roadside graves gaily decked with big irises were a pleasure to behold (Fig. 68).

Kāna, occupied by the Jinkī-khēl clan in its upper and main portion, differs in several ways from other tracts of the Indus Kohistān to which the tide of Pathān invasion has extended. It does not know that mischievous system of *wēsh*, or periodical redistribution of all lands, which elsewhere in this region prevents the undertaking of any permanent improvements. Kāna had not, indeed, escaped that bane of local feuds and vendettas to which the *wēsh* practice contributes so largely. The numerous ruined or deserted dwellings that I saw at Bilkānai were visible proof of this. Yet somehow the people of Kāna had inherited a sense of feudal attachment to their Khāns, and this has evidently helped a good deal towards a ready acceptance of the Bādshāh's new regime.

The two Khāns of Kāna, Amīr Khān and Pīrdād Khān, had been intelligent enough to attach themselves to the cause of the Miāngul long before he gained overlordship. When in 1922 the Pathān clans east of Swāt formed a confederacy to resist the Miāngul's 'forward policy' and gave battle to his invading force in the Mukhozai country, the Khāns kept aloof, though they could not prevent their tribesmen from sharing in the fray and defeat. They had themselves been besieged and had suffered losses. But with the success of the Miāngul they received their reward. Everywhere else he had caused forts and towers of local headmen to be razed to the ground, and had imposed his own trusted servants to manage affairs and enjoy the sweets of office. But his friends, the Khāns of Kāna, had been allowed to keep their forts and to exercise their old quasi-baronial powers in the person of their sons, who were appointed 'Tahsīldārs'.

Naturally enough, both Amīr Khān and Pīrdād Khān were eager to demonstrate their loyalty by a special display of hospitality. So as I travelled down Kāna we were everywhere treated to gay gatherings of their armed retainers, with fluttering banners and much martial music on drum and bagpipe (Fig. 70). It was impossible for me to do due justice to all the festivities prepared at Bar-kāna, Delai, Nawe-kile. But my Swātī protectors and the escort had ample occasion on the way to show their receptive 'capacity'. The quite antique-looking succession of servitors with trays

71. FORT OF DŌST MUḤAMMAD KHĀN OF KĀNA, BILKĀNAI.

72. GHŌRBAND RIVER SPANNED BY SINGLE RAFTER, KARŌRAI.

of viands, large cakes, and sweets could scarcely keep pace with the rapid disposal of their supplies by the big circle of feasting men.

Large-hearted hospitality is one of the best traits in Pathān character, and there could be no doubt about the satisfaction with which old Amīr Khān, a venerable grey-beard, pressed it upon us at Bar-kāna, until the threat of rain forced us to make a timely start for our camping-place lower down under the shelter of the Bādshāh's new castle at Nawe-kile. What pleased me most was the tasteful decoration of the places where we met with this hospitable reception. Glowing red rhododendron blossoms and big white irises were hung on the shrubs and saplings that enclosed them. The rhododendrons were brought down from the mountains, the irises from the burial-grounds on which they grow as abundantly as in Kashmīr.

During my visit to Kāna I enjoyed, perhaps more than anywhere else on this expedition, what seemed like a bodily translation into an earlier phase of human society and life. It is difficult to express clearly in a few words the effect, for one endowed with historical instincts, of close and constant contact with men whose ways of thought and action reflect conditions that the West has left centuries behind. To be able to observe these, unconsciously as it were and undisturbed by the influences of our complex modern life, seemed to me a diverting experience, and at the same time a very instructive lesson in history. The ease with which, under a quasi-medieval regime, all things really needful could be arranged for the favoured few was exemplified in my own case. The advantages thus enjoyed were great indeed and might well explain and excuse a certain reluctance on my part to return to 'civilization' and all its exactions.

By the afternoon of April 25th we had reached the lower

end of the valley of Kāna. We had to take leave of it by two slightly trying river crossings. Both the river of Kāna and that of Ghōrband into which it empties itself near Karōrai are far too deep and rapid to be forded without serious risk. They are bridged both above and below the confluence where rocky defiles confine them. But in both places the bridge actually available consisted of a single big rafter, sagging and swaying a good deal (Fig. 72). It was, I confess, with some relief that I found myself safely on that side of the Ghōrband river which is reckoned in the tribal area of the Azī-khēl centred at Chakēsar. Our route then took us along the steep slopes of the valley which leads straight south up to the range running from the Swāt watershed to the Indus, and after a long ride we reached the village of Upal by nightfall. The 'Sūbahdār' or commandant of Upal met us on the way up to his fort with a large posse of his men-at-arms, who marched, with flags flying, to the weird music of a drum and a bagpipe and enlivened the last stage of our march.

CHAPTER XVI

THE ASCENT TO PĪR-SAR

It was from Upal (Fig. 74), some 5,000 feet above sea-level, that I was to begin the search for a likely site of Aornos. The move necessary for this purpose, along the crest of the range, could only be made on foot. So the mules which had brought our baggage from Kāna were discharged and our riding ponies dispatched across the Upal pass to await us at Chakēsar. I was pleasantly surprised at the ease with which the hundred odd carriers required for our combined camp were collected by the morning of April 26th. But occasional labour of this kind forms part of the conditions of tenure upon which the Gujar and other 'Fakīrs' are allowed to cultivate the land owned by their Azī-khēl masters, and under the prevailing feudal conditions the latter do not seem to find any difficulty in enforcing their claim.

It was a day full of eager expectation, but also not free from anxious uncertainty. On the two preceding nights I had carefully read over the descriptions that Arrian and Curtius have left us of Alexander's great exploit at Aornos. These are detailed enough as regards incidents of the operations by which the formidable rock fastness was captured. But apart from references to the vicinity of the Indus the general topographical indications seemed singularly wanting in precision. Descriptions, in the case of Curtius rhetorically elaborated, of the extent and height of the mountain stronghold and of the difficulties that the attacking Macedonians encountered, could not make up for the lack of exact distances and bearings from definitely known points.

How I wished that the great Alexander had brought in his train some man of letters, accustomed, like a Chinese annalist, to look out for plain topographical facts, such as bearings, distances, and the like, and to record them with impartial clearness alongside of important military events! If he did, we must regret that the fortunes of classical literature have not allowed that record to come down to us. The best I could hope for was to find a ridge or plateau which by its size, position, and configuration would account for the character of the operations that brought about the conquest of the 'Rock'.

All the more grateful did I feel when what proved a long day of physical toil soon brought an encouraging omen. Some 'Kapūr kandare', ruins of heathen (Kāfir) times, had been reported by the greybeards of Upal on a little spur clearly visible from the village and about 1,000 feet above it. I therefore soon left the stony ravine in which our long baggage column was moving towards the summit of the Upal range—as for shortness' sake I may call it—and with my 'handy-man', the ever-agile Shāh 'Ālam, and the escort, climbed up the spur of Chat.

I was rewarded for this detour; for the little plateau on the top showed, not merely the well-cultivated fields of nearly a dozen Gujar households, but also the remains of a small circumvallation which by its characteristic masonry of the 'Gandhāra type' could at once be recognized as dating from the Buddhist period. Search in the fields close by soon brought to light fragments of decorated pottery of the kind which during the preceding weeks I had learned to associate with ancient structures in these parts. Nevertheless, it was a pleasant surprise when Maḥmūd, an intelligent young potter from Upal, who was acting as our guide, picked up under my eyes from below the ruined wall a well-preserved bronze bracelet of unmistakably antique shape and showing a snake head. The rain of the preceding days had loosened the ground and thus prepared the discovery.

73. CREST OF UPAL RANGE SEEN FROM CHAT.

74. UPAL VILLAGE SEEN FROM SOUTH-EAST.

The reward I paid out on the spot, as I always did in such cases, made Maḥmūd beam with joy. But he was, of course, not aware that the ounce of silver was intended also as a return for an important piece of information that he had given me in his talk as we climbed up to Chat. I had been cautiously testing his knowledge about localities farther east on the Upal range and in particular about the high ridge of Pīr-sar, which the Miāngul's people, in response to inquiries started by the Political Agent on the Malakand since I first proposed my tour in search of Aornos, had pointed out as most nearly answering to the broad outlines given them.

Of course Maḥmūd was quite unaware that the great Sultān Sikandar had ever come to these parts; nor did my repeated careful inquiries among local Pathāns, Gujars, and Mullahs reveal the slightest indication that folk-lore or quasi-learned tradition in this region in any way connected Swāt and the adjacent hill tracts with the exploits of Sikandar, the 'two-horned', the legendary hero of the 'Alexander romance' in its Muhammadan version. But in the course of my talk with humble but sharp-witted Maḥmūd I heard for the first time the name of Mount *Ūṇa* mentioned. It was believed by all people, so he said, to be the highest peak on the range that stretches from the pass of Upal to the Indus, and just below it in the direction of the great river lay Pīr-sar, a big alp cherished by the local Gujars as the best of all their 'bāndas' or summer settlements both for grazing and cultivation.

It did not take long for my philological subconsciousness to realize that *Ūṇa* (pronounced with that peculiar cerebral *ṇ* which represents a nasal affected by a preceding or following *r* sound) would be the direct phonetic derivative to be expected, according to strict linguistic evidence, from the Dardic or Sanskrit name that Greek tongues had endeavoured to reproduce by *Aornos*. But, of course, such philological indications could have their weight only if the actual topographical conditions at Pīr-sar were found to agree with those details concerning the siege of Aornos which have been handed down to us from reliable sources.

The eager wish to reach Pīr-sar, if possible, the same day made me think little of the steep climb of some 2,000 feet that carried us from Chat to the crest of the range (Fig. 73). For its upper half it lay through a fine forest of conifers and ilex mixed, with violets and other little messengers of early spring strewing the ground in profusion. We reached the narrow crest of the range at an elevation of close on 8,000 feet, just below the wooded cone whose height had been shown as 8,360 feet by the triangulation effected from across the Indus in the course of the Black Mountain expedition of 1892. The sylvan scenery along the knife-edge crest, which fell away in places in sheer cliffs, was delightful. My eyes feasted once again on the great panorama of snowy mountains to the north, including the noble Mankiāl peaks far away on the horizon (Fig. 75). What with the enjoyment of this charming alpine scenery and the search for a place where the trees would allow photographs to be taken to advantage, the onward march was naturally delayed.

It proved far longer and more trying than I had foreseen. The track, if such it could be called, led along the rocky and precipitous southern face of the range and kept close to its crest with all its ups and downs. I was glad when at last after much scrambling I caught the first view of the Indus valley through the forest. Above it to the south-east I could see the snow-topped heights of the Black Mountains, and far away, beyond a long succession of boldly serrated minor ranges, I could faintly make out the long, undulating

75. SNOWY RANGE BETWEEN GHŌRBAND AND DUBĒR VALLEYS, SEEN FROM CREST OF UPAL RANGE.

outlines of Mahāban. How they revived recollections of my short raid in 1904, which had disproved the identification of that mountain with Aornos! Once again kindly Fate had allowed me to search for the famous 'Rock'. Would it this time grant success?

It was 6 p.m. when we passed a very fine spring gushing forth from the side of the Acharo-sar peak, and after scrambling for another half-mile we reached the open crest of a rocky spur that descends straight from Mount Ūṇa. Just below us spread the grazing alp of 'Little Ūṇa'. And at this point we came in sight of the bare rocky peak of Ūṇa-sar or 'Mount Ūṇa', 8,720 feet high according to the triangulation carried out on the last Black Mountain expedition. Stretching away from it southward the long and flat-topped ridge of Pīr-sar now came into view (Fig. 76). It was a very striking sight, this long and almost level ridge, as it rose there, girt all round with cliffs, above precipitous smaller spurs and steep ravines which were seen to run down to the Indus, over 5,000 feet below. Pīr-sar seemed near enough as I looked across the deep valley, flanked by precipitous slopes mostly bare of tree growth, that separated us from it. But in the end it took us fully three hours more to reach it.

First we had to get past the steep massif of Mount Ūṇa. Its southern face falls away lower down in sheer walls of rock (Fig. 81). We had, therefore, to ascend by a troublesome track following the spur that we had just struck at 'Little Ūṇa'. Climbing along its crest we reached at last a small shoulder, some 200 feet below the actual summit, where it was possible to take to the northern well-wooded side of the mountain. Here the descent began, almost as tiring, along cliffs and steep gullies where the snow still lay thick. It brought us to the small tree-girt alp of Būrimār (Fig. 78), where we found some summer huts of Gujar graziers and the fenced-in resting-place of some Muhammadan saint under fine trees.

At first Būrimār, as sighted from a distance, had seemed to link up with the wooded conical height marking the northern end of the long ridge of Pīr-sar. But now as we passed down the gently sloping grassy alp to its lower edge, I discovered that a deep and precipitous ravine, previously masked by close tree growth, still separated us from that height. It was a surprise, far from pleasant at first sight, for tired men, now that dusk was rapidly coming on. But as under Maḥmūd's guidance we stumbled down among rocks and pines to the bottom of that narrow ravine, fully 600 feet as it proved below the alp, a thought soon began to cheer me. Was this not the deep gap on Aornos which at first baffled the Macedonian attack, after Alexander had joined the detachment sent ahead under Ptolemy, the son of Lagos, near the top of the mountain? There was no time for me then in the growing darkness to examine the ground with reference to the expedient by which, after days of toil, Alexander had managed to bring his slingers and archers sufficiently near the opposite side to reach the defenders with their missiles. When we arrived at last at the bottom of the gully it proved to be a very confined saddle, less than forty yards long and only some ten yards across. Fallen trees encumbered it and also lay thick in the narrow ravines descending on either side. Then my thoughts naturally turned to the 'mound' that Alexander is said to have had constructed with cut trees and stakes across the gap in order to render the assault possible.

We were now at last arrived below the high northern extremity of Pīr-sar itself (Fig. 79)—nor had we to fear the stones and other missiles which an enemy holding the heights would have found it so easy to hurl down. Yet the ascent past the precipitous cliffs lining the south-western

76. PĪR-SAR RIDGE SEEN FROM SOUTH-WESTERN SLOPE OF ŪṆA-SAR PEAK.

77. WESTERN SLOPES OF PĪR-SAR SEEN FROM MĀSHLUN.

slopes of Bar-sar, 'the top hill', as this end of the Pīr-sar ridge is known, was exacting enough for the fatigue of it to be vividly imprinted on my memory. Fortunately towards the end the moon rose sufficiently high to make footholds less difficult to find. But I was heartily glad when at last by 9 p.m. we reached open ground where the flat portion of the ridge adjoins Bar-sar. It was a strange sensation to pass next over nearly a mile of practically level ground, where the full moon shining under a cloudless sky showed verdant fields of young wheat and barley. It served to impress me still more with the remarkable natural features to which this ridge owes its present attractions for the Gujars and which would account for its fame as an ancient mountain refuge.

In the centre of the long flat plateau I found our big camp pitched near a rudely built mosque, at an elevation which subsequent observations showed to be fully 7,100 feet above sea-level. The escort and carriers were gathered round big bonfires, glad of their protection from the bitterly cold wind. It was long after midnight before I could seek warmth amidst my rugs. But the growing conviction that Aornos was found at last kept my spirits buoyant in spite of benumbed hands and weary feet. Alexander, so Arrian and Curtius tell us, offered sacrifices to the gods when he had gained possession of the 'Rock'. I had no victory to give thanks for. Yet I, too, felt tempted to offer a libation to Pallas Athene for the fulfilment of a scholar's hope, long cherished and long delayed.

CHAPTER XVII

IN SEARCH OF AORNOS

It was the search for Aornos that had led me to Pīr-sar. In order to explain the reasons that made me anxious to examine this ground by the Indus with a view to the location of the famous rock fastness, I must turn back to the account of Alexander's campaign where we left it. We have seen that after the capture of Ōra and the subsequent abandonment of Bazira, now confidently located at Bīr-kōṭ, Alexander's operations in the Swāt valley were concluded. Having placed garrisons in these strong places to guard the country, he turned south to rejoin that large division of his army which under Hephaistion and Perdikkas had preceded him down the Kābul river into the open Peshawar valley. Before relating this junction of the Macedonian forces and Alexander's subsequent move to the Indus, Arrian, here as elsewhere our chief authority for all that concerns the great conqueror's campaign, tells us that on hearing of the fall of Ōra, the other Assakēnoi, *i.e.* the people of Swāt, all left their towns and 'fled to the rock in that country called Aornos'.

Arrian then proceeds to inform us of the reason why Alexander was filled with the eager desire to capture that rock fastness. His statements on this point, apart from the topographical indications that they contain, are of general interest for the historical student; for they help to throw welcome light on certain psychological factors that undoubtedly played an important part in more than one of Alexander's wonderful enterprises—just as they did in those of his modern counterpart, Napoleon. At the same time those statements furnish a significant illustration of the critical standpoint from which Arrian was apt to view the fabulous element fostered by the hero of his story. This is what he tells us of Aornos (IV. xxviii).

78. BŪRIMĀR ALP AND SLOPE DOWN TO BŪRIMĀR GULLY, SEEN FROM MĀSHLUN.

79. MĀSHLUN SHOULDER AND BAR-SAR CLIFFS ABOVE, SEEN FROM BELOW BŪRIMĀR.

This is a mighty mass of rock in that part of the country, and a report is current concerning it that even Herakles, the son of Zeus, had found it to be impregnable. Now whether the Theban, or the Tyrian, or the Egyptian Herakles penetrated so far as to the Indians I can neither positively affirm nor deny, but I incline to think that he did not penetrate so far; for we know how common it is for men when speaking of things that are difficult to magnify the difficulty by declaring that it would baffle even Herakles himself. And in the case of this rock my own conviction is that Herakles was mentioned to make the story of its capture all the more wonderful. The rock is said to have had a circuit of about 200 stadia, and at its lowest elevation a height of 11 stadia. It was ascended by a single path cut by the hand of man, yet difficult. On the summit of the rock there was, it is also said, plenty of pure water which gushed out from a copious spring. There was timber besides, and as much good arable land as required for its cultivation the labour of a thousand men.

Alexander on learning these particulars was seized with an ardent desire to capture this mountain also, the story current about Herakles not being the least of the incentives.

We may never know whether the ambition stimulated by such reports about Aornos was the sole incentive that decided Alexander to effect its capture. The decision was probably due quite as much, if not more, to the strategic principle invariably kept in view by Alexander of never leaving an enemy behind him until he had been completely crushed. Anyhow, we have seen that instead of pursuing the fugitive Assakĕnoi to their mountain retreat, Alexander moved from Swăt into the Peshawar valley. There he organized the Macedonian control over this important district and then proceeded to the Indus.

Arrian does not explicitly tell us that Aornos was situated on the left bank of the Indus. But the narratives of Diodorus and Curtius agree in distinctly indicating this position, and there are strong reasons for looking for Aornos there. I have set them forth fully elsewhere, and a brief summary will here suffice. In the first place a glance at the map will show that with Macedonian posts established up the main Swāt valley as far as the vicinity of Mingaora, the bulk of the fugitive population evacuating the towns farther up the valley could seek safety neither to the west nor to the south.

In the former direction the way was obviously barred by the invaders. To the south, as far as it could be reached by routes not commanded by the Macedonian posts guarding the main valley, there lay Bunēr, a country singularly open for the most part and accessible by numerous passes from the Peshawar valley. This had already been reached by the major portion of Alexander's army, and thus Bunēr, too, lay open to invasion. Turning to the north, no safe refuge from invasion could be hoped for in that portion of the main Swāt valley, which, as we have seen, continues remarkably open and easy as far as Churrai, and the same applies to the side valleys that open from this portion. Higher up, in the narrow gorges of Tōrwāl, invasion would, no doubt, be kept off by the natural difficulties of the ground. But there, no less than at the alpine heads of the valleys descending from the high watersheds towards the Panjkōra and Indus, local resources would have been far too limited for the maintenance of a great host of fugitives.

Conditions were far more favourable for a retreat to the east. Here the large and for the most part fertile tracts of Ghōrband, Kāna, Pūran, Mukhozai, stretching down to the Indus, could be reached by several easy passes, open throughout the year, leading across the watershed from the Swāt side to Ghōrband. By crossing the range towards the Indus the fugitives would place a natural barrier between themselves and the invaders. Behind it they would find local resources amply sufficient for their maintenance until the danger had passed. And, finally, with secure access to the Indus they would have there the advantage of being able to draw help from across the river or else to continue their retreat in that direction.

The great importance of this advantage becomes obvious when we remember what Arrian has previously told us about the help which the defenders of Ōra had expected from Abisares, the chief whose power extended over the present Hazāra and adjacent valleys to the left bank of the Indus where it faces the lower portions of the tracts above named. There is plenty of historical evidence down to quite modern times to attest the close relations between Swāt and this territory to the east of the Indus. The population of Hazāra is largely composed of a tribe still known as Swātīs, descended from the pre-Muhammadan inhabitants of Swāt whom the Pathān invasion of the late Middle Ages had driven out of their original seats. Equally significant is the fact that the Pathān clans now settled on both the Swāt and Hazāra sides of the river, and closely allied in descent, have always shared in the fighting which attended the several Black Mountain expeditions since the British annexation of the Panjāb.

Thus we have converging evidence to explain why the retreat of the inhabitants of Upper Swāt had led them eastwards to the Indus. At the same time it helps us to understand the sound strategic reasons which caused Alexander, before attacking Aornos, first to turn south to the Peshawar valley. Once he had consolidated his hold there and made his arrangements for crossing the Indus quite secure, he could safely move up its right bank and attack the mountain retreat of the Swāt fugitives from the south. He thus avoided the entanglement in a mountainous region that would have attended and hampered direct pursuit from the Swāt side. The fugitive host could be cut off from retreat to the east of the Indus and from such assistance as Abisares, the ruler on that side, might offer. Finally, when attacking Aornos from the south, Alexander could command all the advantages which the Indus valley and the fertile plains of the Peshawar valley would offer in respect of supplies and other resources.

The importance of this last consideration is clearly brought out by what Arrian tells us after briefly recording that Alexander, having put a Macedonian garrison into the city of Peukelaotis (Sanskrit Pushkalāvatī), the ancient capital of Gandhāra, located at the present Chārsadda north-east of Peshawar, moved eastwards and 'reduced other towns, some small ones situated on the Indus'.

> After he had arrived at Embolima, which town lay not far from the rock of Aornos, he there left Krateros with a portion of the army to collect into the town as much corn as possible and all other requisites for a prolonged stay, in order that the Macedonians having that place as a base might by protracted investment wear out those holding the rock, in case it were not taken at the first assault. He himself taking with him the archers, the Agrianians, the brigade of Koinos, the lightest and best armed from the rest of the phalanx, two hundred of the companion cavalry and a hundred mounted archers, marched to the rock.

Arrian does not indicate the exact position of Embolima. But since we have seen that Aornos was situated on the right bank of the Indus, the town chosen to serve as Alexander's base of supplies may with good reason be also looked for there. The mention made in Ptolemy's *Geography* of Embolima as a town of Indo-Scythia situated on the Indus confirms this. But neither the Greek geographer's notice nor the mention of the same place under its Sanskrit name *Ambulima* in that quaint Buddhist text, the *Geography of the Demons*, to which I had occasion to refer in connexion with the blankets of Churrai, helps us to determine the exact position of Embolima.

When General Abbott, the valiant Frontier Officer from whom Abbottabad, the administrative centre of Hazāra, takes its name, discussed in 1854 his location of Aornos on the Mahāban range south of Bunēr, he proposed, as M. Court, one of Ranjit Singh's French generals had done before him in 1839, to recognize Embolima in the present village of Amb situated on the right bank of the Indus. It lies about eight miles to the east of Mahāban and is the place from which the Nawāb of Amb, one of the Miāngul's recent antagonists, takes his title. This identification of Aornos with Mahāban had been proposed without a visit to the locality—then wholly inaccessible to any European—and was based mainly on what the telescope used from a great distance on the Hazāra side of the river was believed to show. This identification had proved untenable in the light of the true topographical features of the supposed site, as revealed by the close survey of Mahāban carried out by me in 1904.

This fact did not necessarily invalidate the location of Embolima at Amb. But even if it is accepted, though resting solely on the identity of the modern name with the first syllable of Embolima—philologically weak evidence since the apocope of fully three syllables at the end is difficult to account for—we are still left free to look for Aornos higher up on the Indus; for Arrian's narrative shows that it took Alexander two marches from Embolima to reach the neighbourhood of Aornos. Already, when recording the conclusive evidence furnished by my visit to Mahāban in 1904 against the conjectured location of Aornos on that range, I had realized that we must look for the site farther up the great river. But as that tribal territory remained inaccessible, it was not until fourteen years later that my attention was definitely drawn to an area where a probable solution of the problem might be looked for.

A very valuable clue was then furnished by my friend, the late Colonel R. A. Wauhope, R.E., a highly accomplished officer of the Survey of India, whom the Great War had temporarily brought back from retirement to the Trigonometrical Survey Office at Dehra Dun. Work was then proceeding on the maps reproducing the surveys carried out on my three Central-Asian expeditions. Colonel Wauhope had been in charge of the survey operations conducted on the left bank of the Indus during the Black Mountain campaigns of 1888 and 1891–2. From high survey stations then established on the Black Mountain range and again during the brief occupation of the tribal tracts of Nandihār and Allāhī farther north, he had become familiar with the general features of the Indus valley below and the hills overlooking it on the opposite side, all the way from above Amb to Chakēsar. Remaining a sound classical scholar all though his life, he was interested in the question of Aornos. From his observations at that time he had come to conclude that a position corresponding to that described by Alexander's historians was more likely to be found on the mountain spurs descending steeply to the Indus opposite to the mouth of the Nandihār valley near Thākōt than anywhere else. But his experience as a topographer had also told him that only by close examination on the spot could a definite location be hoped for.

From what the available map of the Survey of India showed of this region, which had then been roughly sketched from a distance, there could be no doubt that the spurs referred to by Colonel Wauhope were the easternmost finger-like offshoots of the range that trends with a due easterly bearing and a total length of close on twenty miles from the Swāt-Indus watershed to the Indus and divides the Ghōrband valley from Chakēsar. That this range drops very steeply towards the river, which flows round its foot in a sharp bend, was evident enough from the short distance that the map showed between the highest triangulated point

80. VIEW OF SNOWY RANGE AT HEAD OF SWĀT VALLEY, LOOKING NORTH FROM LĀNDE-SAR.

High peaks above Mankiāl are seen to right.

81. ŪṆA-SAR PEAK SEEN FROM KUZ-SAR.

Little Ūṇa and Achar alps on slopes to left, Balai on spur below them; Būrimār on right. View beyond Būrimār is continued on left of Fig. 82.

on its crest and the river-bed at Thākōt, fully 7,000 feet lower. I could gather little else from the map regarding the topography of the high ground that we had gained in the dark by our trying march to Pīr-sar. All the more eagerly did I long for the morning which was to reveal it in full clearness.

CHAPTER XVIII

THE SURVEY OF PĪR-SAR

THE violent gusts of wind that shook my little tent during the night of my arrival on Pīr-sar left but a poor chance of sleep before I rose next morning at daybreak. The view that spread before me at this well-detached height of some 7,100 feet above sea-level was extraordinarily wide and grand. But the icy blasts blowing down the Indus from the snow-covered ranges of the Kohistān, comparatively so near, made it difficult to enjoy it fully until midday had brought calm and warmth. It was the same throughout the three days that we spent on this exposed height. None the less I found the work during these days most fascinating, favoured as it was by continuous clear weather. The task involved a detailed survey of Pīr-sar and the whole region around it, supplemented by whatever information could be gathered about practicable routes, cultivation, water-supply, and other local conditions.

It was in the course of the close survey unremittingly pursued during this period that I realized more and more clearly that striking agreement of topographical features which brought the conviction that in this remarkable ridge of Pīr-sar we have indeed the long-sought-for rock fastness of Aornos. The sketch-map reproduced from the plane-table survey that Surveyor Tōrabāz Khān prepared under my supervision on the large scale of four inches to the mile, together with the photographs (Figs. 76–86), will help to illustrate these features. Yet some description of details is needed before we proceed to review the records left to us of Alexander's siege of Aornos and to examine the relevant details of this story in the light of the topographical knowledge acquired.

Pīr-sar is but one of a series of narrow spurs which the

82. NORTHERN END OF PĪR-SAR RIDGE WITH BAR-SAR AND LĀNDE-SAR ABOVE; SWĀT-INDUS WATERSHED RANGE IN DISTANCE.

On the left where the view joins the right edge of the one shown in Fig. 81 are seen the lower slope of Būrimār and the Māshlun shoulder. On the right the view extends across the Dratserge ridge and the Ghōrband valley.

range stretching east from above Upal throws out to the south before it drops rapidly and flattens out fanlike towards the low plateau of Maira washed at its foot by the Indus. Of these spurs Pīr-sar preserves its height for the longest distance, and owing to the uniform level and the very fertile soil of its summit affords most scope both for cultivation and grazing. The practically level portion of the top (Fig. 85) extends at an average elevation of about 7,100 feet for over a mile and a half. At its upper end this flat portion is bordered for some distance by gentle slopes equally suited for such use (Fig. 82).

Owing to its greater height and the depth of the valleys on either side Pīr-sar forms a dominating position; overlooking all the other spurs, it offers an exceptionally wide and impressive view. This comprises the whole of the Indus valley from below the Mahāban range in the south to where the winding course of the great river lies hidden between closely packed spurs descending from the high snowy ranges towards Kāghān and the Swāt headwaters (Fig. 87). To give some idea of the extent of the vast panorama commanded from Pīr-sar I may mention that it includes northward the great ice-crowned peaks above Tōrwāl, Dubēr, and Kandia (Fig. 80), and to the east all the ranges that adjoin the central part of Hazāra. Southward the plain of the Peshawar valley above Attock could be distinctly seen.

The spur from its level top, to which the name *Pīr-sar*, 'the holy man's height', is properly applied, falls away both on the east and west in very steep rocky slopes (Fig. 77). In places these form sheer cliffs, while in others pines and firs have managed to secure a footing. The southern end of Pīr-sar rises into a small but conspicuous hillock, known as Kuz-sar, 'the lower height', as opposed to the Bar-sar at the northern end (Fig. 82). There the spur divides into three narrow branches, all flanked by precipitous rocky slopes (Fig. 83). The crest of the middle one is in its upper portion so steep and narrow as to be practically inaccessible. The shortest branch, called Māju, juts out like a bastion to the south-west, before it terminates in sheer cliffs at a level of about 1,600 feet below the top of Pīr-sar.

The western slope of Pīr-sar descends steeply for some 2,000 feet into a very confined valley (Fig. 77). The bottom of this forms in parts an impracticable ravine, while in others little terraces bear a few scattered fields. On the opposite side of the valley rises the small spur of Balai, flanked by formidable bare cliffs, almost perpendicular in places. There are short stretches of more gentle slope on its summit, which are used for summer grazing; but these are practically accessible only from the crest of the main range just below the Ūṇa-sar peak. A deep ravine divides the spur of Balai westwards from another and much longer one, known to the local Gujars as Danda-Nūrdai. This detaches itself from the main range near the grazing-grounds of Lāndai and farther down faces the south-western slopes of Pīr-sar.

Its narrow serrated crest is crossed by two passes. The lower one, called Pēzal-kandao, with an elevation of about 4,000 feet, gives access to a portion of the valley where opposite to the cliffs of Māju some cultivation is carried on by the scattered homesteads of the Gujar hamlet of Tālun. From below the Pēzal-kandao it is possible to ascend by a difficult track to the crest of the Māju spur, and thence to the southern end of Pīr-sar. Across the other pass, about 6,500 feet above sea-level, a somewhat easier route leads from the valley behind the Danda-Nūrdai spur to the grassy slopes below the alp of Little Ūṇa, and thence joins the track passing along the top of the main range. We shall see below that these passes may claim some interest in connexion with the story of Aornos.

83. CLIFFS BELOW KUZ-SAR END OF PĪR-SAR, SEEN FROM ASHARAI RIDGE.

From here we must turn back to Pīr-sar to acquaint ourselves rapidly with the ground which adjoins it to the east. That it differs in some respects from that observed to the west is due mainly to the fact that the main range, after throwing off to the south the commanding spur of Pīr-sar, very soon falls off in height and becomes bare of trees. The drainage here gathers in one wide trough before taking its course to the Indus. Between the deeply eroded Nullahs that join this trough there rises a succession of short knolls and ridges. All have very steep slopes, but are crowned by little plateaux which, as seen from Pīr-sar, give them an appearance curiously suggestive of small detached islands (Fig. 84). Some of these little hill-tops bear patches of cultivation; but all are devoid of trees and water, and only capable of temporary occupation. The slopes of Pīr-sar facing east also descend very steeply.

It only remains to describe briefly the summit of the Pīr-sar spur. This presents itself for a distance of a little over a mile and a half as an almost level plateau, occupied along practically its whole length by fields of wheat. The width of the cultivated ground on the top varies from about 100 to 200 yards, with strips available for grazing by the side of the fields. Fine old trees form small groves in places (Fig. 85), and one of these near the middle of the ridge shelters a much-frequented Ziārat, or shrine. There are several small springs in the little gullies that furrow the steep slopes close below the ridge, and these feed the streams that drain into the valleys below. But, in addition, two large reservoirs have been constructed of *bands* of rough stonework to store a large supply of water from rain or melting snow, and thus to meet the need of the herds of cattle that are brought to graze here during the summer months. We found them filled to a depth of several feet.

Over two dozen homesteads, roughly built in the Gujar

fashion, and scattered in groups over the plateau, serve to shelter the families that move up with their cattle and occupy Pīr-sar from late spring till the autumn. The mosque that I shall presently refer to forms the centre of the settlement. Owing to the fact that the Pīr-sar ridge stretches from north to south and is nowhere shaded by higher ground, its summit receives an abundance of sunshine. It consequently becomes clear of snow very early in the year. This explains also why, in spite of an abnormally late spring, we found the wheat already standing high.

At its southern end Pīr-sar is guarded, as it were, by the hill of Kuz-sar already mentioned, which rises about 100 feet above the plateau and completely commands the difficult paths leading up from the Māju and Asharai crests. At the northern extremity the plateau is still more effectively protected by the bold conical hill of Bar-sar, which rises to a height of about 7,900 feet, and is thus at its summit about 800 feet higher than the plateau. The approach from the latter to the thickly wooded top lies first over easy grassy slopes (Fig. 82), but for about the last 300 feet becomes very steep and rocky. The top portion of Bar-sar has a distinctly triangular shape. It is fringed with crags along each of its sides and these are very precipitous except at the angle pointing north. There an easier slope leads down 200 feet to a narrow saddle, and close beyond it rises a small flat-topped outlier of Bar-sar known as Lānde-sar, 'the lower height' (Fig. 80). Its elevation is but little less than that of Bar-sar, and the slopes below it are very steep and rocky.

It is by the angle pointing west that Bar-sar joins up with the main range, in the axial line of which it lies. But it is just here that the continuity of the range is broken by the deep and precipitous ravine that we encountered on our

84. RIDGES OF DRATSERGE AND BĒNAMĀZ TO EAST OF PĪR-SAR, SEEN FROM LĀNDE-SAR.

first approach to Pīr-sar. The bottom of this ravine lies approximately on the same level as the plateau of Pīr-sar and about 600 feet below the alp of Būrimār which, as we have seen, faces Bar-sar. I have already described the troublesome descent from Būrimār to the bottom of the ravine known as Būrimār-kandao. But the angle at which the narrow rocky *arête* from the top of Bar-sar runs down to it is still steeper.

The succession of crags, in places almost vertical, is here, however, broken at one point by a small projecting shoulder, called *Māshlun*. This, visible in Fig. 79, is quite flat on its top and extends for about half a furlong westwards, with a width of some thirty yards at its end. Trees grow on it thickly, as they do also on the rocky slopes above and below. This shoulder of Māshlun juts out at a height of about 450 feet above the bottom of the ravine, and behind it precipitous cliffs rise for another 350 feet or so higher to the summit of Bar-sar. To the remains of an ancient fort traceable on this summit, and to the important topographical indication presented by the shoulder of Māshlun, I shall presently recur.

Having now described the actual configuration, I may briefly sum up the essential features that necessarily in vested it with exceptional advantages as a place of safety and natural stronghold for the ancient inhabitants of this region. Its great elevation, more than 5,000 feet above the Indus, would alone make attack difficult. The extent of level space on its top, greater than that to be found on any height of equal natural strength farther down on the right bank of the Indus, would permit of the assembly of large numbers both for safety and for defence. Its central position would make Pīr-sar a particularly convenient rallying-place for large and fertile hill tracts such as Chakēsar and Ghōrband, as well as for that portion of the Indus valley lying close below, where the space available for cultivation is wide and villages accordingly large and numerous.

The great height and steepness of the slopes with which Pīr-sar is girt would suffice to make its defence easy in times when those fighting from a superior height had every physical advantage on their side. And in this respect full account must also be taken of the fact that even on the side where the spur adjoins and is overlooked by the main range, it is isolated by the deep ravine of the Būrimār-kandao. Nor should the great strategic strength of the general position be overlooked, considering that over two-thirds of it, as the map shows, are protected by the great bend of the Indus.

CHAPTER XIX

THE STORY OF ALEXANDER'S SIEGE OF AORNOS

FROM our survey of Pīr-sar we may now turn back to the record of Alexander's operations where we left it on his arrival in the vicinity of Aornos. Among the extant accounts of Alexander's great feat there, that of Arrian (*Anabasis*, IV. xxix–xxx) is the fullest and also undoubtedly the most reliable. We may attach all the more value to it in the present connexion because, of the two contemporary authorities whose narratives Arrian in his preface declares to be worthy of more credit than all the rest, one was that same Ptolemy, son of Lagos and the first of the Ptolemies of Egypt, who personally played a very important part in the conquest of Aornos. Arrian's account of the operations which led to the capture of the rock fastness of the fugitive Assakēnoi is so clear and instructive in its topographical details that it seems best to reproduce Mr. McCrindle's translation of it *in extenso*, with a few slight alterations which an examination of the original text appears to me to render necessary.

Some men thereupon who belonged to the neighbourhood came to him, and after proffering their submission undertook to guide him to the place most suited for an attack upon the rock, that from which it would not be difficult to capture the place. With these men he sent Ptolemy, the son of Lagos, and a member of the bodyguard, leading the Agrianians and the other light-armed troops and the selected hypaspists, and directed him, on securing the position, to hold it with a strong guard and signal to him when he had occupied it. Ptolemy, following a route which was trying and difficult, secured the position without being perceived by the barbarians. He fortified this all round with a palisade and a trench, and then raised a beacon on that part of the mountain from which it could be seen by Alexander.

The signal fire was seen, and next day Alexander moved forward with his army; but as the barbarians offered valiant opposition he could do nothing more owing to the difficult nature of the ground. When the barbarians perceived that Alexander had found an attack [on that side] to be impracticable, they turned round and attacked Ptolemy's men. Between these and the Macedonians hard fighting ensued, the Indians making strenuous efforts to destroy the palisade and Ptolemy to hold the position. The barbarians had the worse in the skirmish, and when night fell withdrew.

From the Indian deserters Alexander selected one who knew the country and could otherwise be trusted, and sent him by night to Ptolemy with a letter importing that when he himself assailed the rock, Ptolemy should not content himself with holding his position but should fall upon the barbarians on the mountain, so that the Indians, being attacked on both sides, might be perplexed how to act. Alexander, starting at daybreak from his camp, led his army to that approach by which Ptolemy had ascended unobserved, being convinced that if he forced a passage that way and effected a junction with Ptolemy's men, the work still before him would not be difficult.

And so it turned out; for up to midday there continued hard fighting between the Indians and Macedonians, the latter forcing their way up while the former plied them with missiles as they ascended. But as the Macedonians did not slacken their efforts, others succeeding to others, while those [before] in advance rested, they gained with trouble the pass in the afternoon and joined Ptolemy's men. The troops being now all united were thence put again in motion towards the rock itself; but an assault upon it was still impracticable. So came this day to its end.

Next day at dawn he ordered the soldiers to cut a hundred stakes per man. When the stakes had been cut he began from the top of the height on which they were encamped, to pile up towards the rock a great mound, whence he thought it would be possible for arrows and for missiles shot from engines to reach the defenders. Every one took part in the work, helping to pile up the mound. He himself was present to superintend, commending those that with eagerness advanced the work, and chastising any one that at the moment was idling.

The army on that first day extended the mound the length of a stadion. On the following day the slingers, by slinging stones at the Indians from the mound just constructed, and the bolts shot from the engines drove back the sallies made by the Indians on those engaged upon the mound. The work of piling it up went on for three days, without intermission. On the fourth day a few Macedonians had forced their way to and secured a small hillock level with the rock. Alexander without ever resting drove the mound forward, intending to join the mound to the hillock which the handful of men already held for him.

But the Indians, terror-struck at the unheard-of audacity of the Macedonians who had forced their way to the hillock, and on seeing the mound already connected with it, abstained from further resistance, and sending their herald to Alexander, professed their willingness to surrender the rock if he would treat for peace with them. But the purpose they had in view was to consume the day in spinning out negotiations, and to disperse by night to their several homes. When Alexander perceived this he gave them time to start off as well as to withdraw the round of sentries everywhere. He himself remained quiet until they began their retreat; and then he took with him seven hundred of the bodyguard and of the hypaspists and was the first to scale the rock where it had been abandoned. The Macedonians climbed up after him, pulling one another up, some at one place, some at another. And then at a preconcerted signal they turned upon the retreating barbarians and slew many of them in the flight; some others retreating in terror flung themselves down the precipices and died. Alexander thus became master of the rock which had baffled Herakles himself.

With this clear, sober, and full record of Arrian the accounts given by Diodorus and Curtius agree in all essential topographical points. That these two authors used common sources here as elsewhere is evident from various indications. But Diodorus contents himself with a much-condensed abstract, and Curtius' narrative owes its greater length mainly to his usual expansion of such minor aspects of the story as specially lend themselves to rhetorical treatment. It will therefore be sufficient, in either account, to note only those points which have a bearing on the location of Aornos.

Diodorus (*Bibliotheca*, XVII. lxxxv) describes the 'Rock' as a natural stronghold, 100 stadia in circumference, 16 stadia in height, and with a level surface forming a complete circle. The Indus washed its foot on the south; elsewhere it was surrounded by deep ravines and inaccessible cliffs.

An old man familiar with the neighbourhood promised, for a reward, to take Alexander up the difficult ascent to a position which would command the barbarians in occupation of the 'Rock'. Guided by him, Alexander first seized the pass leading to the 'Rock', and as there was no other exit from it, blocked up the barbarians. He then filled up the ravine which lay at the foot of the 'Rock' with a mound, and thus getting nearer, vigorously pushed the siege by assaults continued without intermission during seven days and nights. At first the barbarians had the advantage owing to the greater height of their position. But when the mound was completed and catapults and other engines had been brought into action, the Indians were struck with despair and escaped from the 'Rock' at night by the pass from which Alexander had on purpose withdrawn the guard previously placed there. Thus Alexander secured the 'Rock' without risk.

Curtius (*Historiae*, VIII. xi) in his description of the 'Rock' (*petra*), which he calls by the name of *Aornis*, does not give any dimensions but mentions that the Indus, deep and confined between steep banks, washes its foot. Elsewhere there were ravines and craggy precipices. In rhetorical style, apparently inspired by a reminiscence of Livy, Curtius likens the 'Rock' to the *meta* of the Roman circus, 'which has a wide base, tapers off in ascending, and terminates in a sharp pinnacle'. This description, if it is based on some passage of his original source, would suggest that one portion of the 'Rock' rose into a steep conical point. We are told that under the guidance of an old man from the neighbourhood a light-armed detachment was sent ahead by a detour to occupy the highest summit unobserved by the enemy.

Curtius next relates that in order to make an assault practicable a ravine was filled up with a mound. For this the trees of a forest close at hand were cut down and their trunks, stripped of branches and leaves, thrown in. By the seventh day the hollows had been filled. An assault up the steep slopes by the archers and Agriani was then ordered. Thirty selected youths from among the king's pages under Charus and Alexander formed the forlorn hope. In the highly rhetorical description that follows it is, however, the king himself who is said to have taken the lead in the assault. Many are said to have perished, falling from the steep crags into the river that flowed below, 'since the barbarians rolled down huge stones upon those climbing up, and such as were struck by them fell headlong from their insecure and slippery footing'. A long and poetical account is then given of the death of the two leaders, Charus and Alexander, who had got up high enough to engage in hand-to-hand fighting, but were overpowered and fell.

The king, affected by these losses, then ordered the retreat, which was carried out in an orderly fashion. Alexander, though resolved to abandon the enterprise, yet made demonstrations of continuing the siege. Thereupon the Indians, with a show of confidence and even triumph, feasted for two days and two nights, but on the third night abandoned the 'Rock'. When their retirement was discovered, the king ordered his troops to raise a general shout. This struck such terror into the fugitives that many, 'flinging themselves headlong over the slippery rocks and precipices', were killed or were left behind injured.

The three accounts translated or analysed above are the only ones that we possess that furnish any specific data about Aornos. From a comparison of them we can deduce the following definite indications as regards the locality referred to. Aornos was a natural stronghold, situated on a mountain of great height, rendered capable of easy defence against an aggressor by precipitous rocky slopes and deep-cut valleys below it. It is important to note that no mention is made anywhere of fortification by the hand of man. There was sufficient level space on the top to permit of considerable numbers finding there a safe refuge. The site was near to the Indus, which flowed at its foot. Its relative height must have been very striking to account for the definite measurements of 11 and 16 stadia, approximately corresponding to 6,600 or 9,600 feet, recorded by Arrian and Diodorus respectively. In the same way the circuits of 200 and 100 stadia mentioned by these two authors, approximately corresponding to 22 and 11 miles, can obviously apply only to a mountain massif or range and not to a single hill or peak.

That Aornos was situated on such a massif or range is in fact made perfectly clear by what all three authors relate of the commanding height occupied by the Macedonians before the beginning of the siege and reached after an arduous ascent. Both Arrian and Curtius state that the march by which the light-armed detachment sent ahead by Alexander secured this position under local guidance remained unobserved by the enemy. This distinctly suggests that the route followed led up a valley that was hidden from the view of the defenders of Aornos.

This assumption finds strong support in Arrian's reference to the pass to which Alexander, when subsequently following the same difficult route, had to ascend amidst severe fighting, before he could join Ptolemy's detachment holding the position above Aornos. Incidentally the opposition here encountered by Alexander indicates that this route leading to the summit of the range, though not visible from Aornos and hence not obstructed on the first occasion, was yet accessible to its defenders without their having first to dislodge the detachment on the height. We learn from Arrian that an attempt to dislodge it had in fact been made on the preceding day but had failed.

We come now to the most significant among the topographical features recorded in connexion with Alexander's siege of Aornos: I refer to the deep ravine separating the heights on which stood the Macedonian camp from the nearest part of the 'Rock'. Here, too, Arrian's account is the fullest and clearest. It shows us that the primary object for which Alexander had to resort to the expedient of constructing a great mound across the ravine was to bring the opposite slope held by the enemy within effective range of what by an anachronism might be called the small arms and field artillery of his force. The precipitous nature of that slope would lend itself to easy and most effective defence, in particular by rolling down large stones, a formidable method of defence the actual use of which Curtius here specially mentions. We find a very striking illustration of the results which in modern times have attended this means of defence on alpine ground in the achievement of the valiant bands of Tyrolese peasants who successfully protected their country in 1809 from invasion by Napoleon's French and Bavarian troops. No assault could succeed against Aornos until 'it would be possible for arrows and for missiles shot from engines to reach the defenders'.

We obtain some indication of the great width of the ravine, and indirectly also of its depth, from Arrian's statements concerning the construction of this mound. By the united efforts of the troops it was extended on the first day the length of a stadion, *i.e.* about 600 feet. After this it became possible, by means of slingers posted on the mound and by shots from the engines, to drive back sallies made against those engaged on the construction of the mound. But 'the work of piling it up went on for three days without intermission' before an assault made on the fourth enabled a handful of Macedonians to establish themselves on 'a small hill which was on a level with the rock'.

Yet even after this, we are told by Arrian, the construction of the mound was continued until it was joined up with the position thus gained. This position must have lain still considerably below the crest of the height that faced the ravine from the side of the 'Rock'. Thus only is it possible to account for the stiff climb which it cost Alexander and his selected seven hundred to reach the top and fall upon the retreating barbarians during the night following their offer of surrender.

CHAPTER XX

AORNOS LOCATED ON PĪR-SAR

Our survey as recorded in the map and the preceding description have made it easy to recognize, in the local features of Pīr-sar and its environs, all the topographical details of Aornos as they appear from the account of Alexander's siege. Taking the general features first, we see from the map that the Indus flows in a wide bend round that eastern extremity of the range of which the Pīr-sar spur is the largest and most conspicuous offshoot. The more specific statement of Diodorus that the Indus washed the rock on its southern side is borne out by the map, which shows that the portion of this bend which a force coming up the Indus valley would first reach lies due south of Pīr-sar.

The relative elevation of Bar-sar at the northern end of the spur (7,914 feet by clinometer), if measured from the bank of the Indus (about 1,700 feet at Thākōt), agrees remarkably well with the height of Aornos, 11 stadia or about 6,600 feet, as recorded by Arrian. If the relative height of the Ūṇa peak (8,721 feet above sea-level by triangulation) is taken, the agreement becomes, if anything, still closer. Obviously no such test can be applied to the measurement of the circuit, for we do not know on what lines or on which level it was taken. It is curious to note that if a map measurer is passed round the foot of the eastern extremity of the range from near Sarkul on the Indus past the Takhta pass to Shang and thence back again behind the Ūṇa peak we get a total direct length of some twenty-two miles. But, of course, other measurements, greater or lesser, would also be possible.

Coming next to the commanding height near Aornos which a light-armed force was sent ahead under Ptolemy to occupy, it is clear that the small plateaux on either flank of Mount Ūṇa would exactly answer the purpose in view. This was to secure a position on that side from which the 'Rock' was most assailable. Taking into account all the tactical advantages that the possession of higher ground must have given the assailant, before the invention of long-range fire-arms even more than in later times, there can be no doubt that the side whence an attack upon the rock-girt plateau of Pīr-sar would offer most chances of success would be where the spur was attached to, and overlooked by, the main range. This is the Būrimār plateau on the eastern shoulder of the culminating peak of Ūṇa-sar (Fig. 78).

But there are considerations which incline me to favour the gently sloping alp of 'Little Ūṇa' immediately below the western flank of Ūṇa-sar as the most likely site of Ptolemy's fortified encampment. From here it was easier to guard the route leading up from the river, and thus to give that support to the subsequent ascent of the main force which Arrian's account shows to have become indispensable once the defenders had discovered the Macedonian move. 'Little Ūṇa' offers also the advantage, at any rate to-day, of easier access to water, and by its situation it was less exposed to attack from the enemy's main position on Pīr-sar.

The route by which the crest of the range where it overlooks Pīr-sar could best be gained from the river certainly led up the valley to the west of the Danda-Nūrdai spur, and thence from the head of the valley to 'Little Ūṇa'. The information collected by me showed that this route is considered the easiest by which the grazing-grounds on the top of the main range can be reached from that side. It is regularly used by the local Gujars when moving to those pastures from their hamlets above the Indus. Near the head of the valley the pass shown in the map as having a clinometrical height of 6,741 feet gives access to the lower slopes of 'Little Ūṇa', and from these the alps occupied by the Gujar huts of Achar and Little Ūṇa can be gained without difficulty.

It is the route just described that I believe, for the reasons indicated, to have been followed first by Ptolemy and then also by Alexander's main column. Arrian tells us that after Alexander had seen the beacon lit by Ptolemy on the mountain he had occupied, he next day moved forward with his troops, but as his progress was obstructed by the barbarians, 'he could do nothing more owing to the difficult nature of the ground'. Reference to the map will show how easy it was for the enemy collected on Pīr-sar to obstruct Alexander's march up that valley once Ptolemy's preceding move had been discovered and had indicated the direction which Alexander's attack was likely to take. The valley west of the Danda-Nūrdai spur is within easy reach from the south-western outlier of Pīr-sar across the heights above the pass known as Pēzal-kandao, 4,620 feet above sea-level. By crowning these heights the enemy could seriously interfere with the advance of the Macedonians up the valley, without risking a battle in the open. It was equally easy for them, when Alexander's advance up the valley had been brought to a standstill, to turn round and, moving higher up, to attack Ptolemy's detachment holding the fortified camp, which, as we have seen, may be placed at or near Little Ūṇa.

This attack was beaten off, and when Alexander on the next day resumed his advance up the valley, the Indians who contested it were attacked in the rear by Ptolemy, to whom Alexander during the night had managed to send orders to this effect, as recorded by Arrian. The importance of this help, as well as the difficulties encountered by Alexander, can be well understood by looking at the map. Not until the pass marked there with the height of 6,741 feet had been taken could the junction with Ptolemy's force be effected, and considering its elevation and the steepness of the Danda-Nūrdai spur, Arrian's description of the severe struggle required to gain it cannot have been exaggerated.

Once the Macedonian forces were united in the course of the afternoon the further advance towards the 'Rock', which Arrian mentions as having been made during the remainder of the day, could present no difficulty. This advance would necessarily lie along the crest of the range as far as the Būrimār plateau. That it came to a standstill, as Arrian records, without any attack on the 'Rock' being for the moment possible, is fully explained by the great natural obstacle met beyond, the fosse of the Būrimār ravine.

I have already described the general character of this ravine, its considerable depth, and the precipitous nature of its slopes. But in order to realize better how fully its features explain Alexander's resort to the construction of a mound for the purpose of crossing it, attention must be called to some details. I have referred above to the protection afforded to Pīr-sar by the extremely steep rocky slopes stretching from the Bar-sar hill, its northern bastion, down towards the ravine, some 800 feet below, that separates it from Būrimār. These slopes, so easily defended from above, could not be attacked with any chance of success unless they could be brought within the range of missiles. Now the direct distance separating the top of Bar-sar from ground of approximately the same level on the Būrimār plateau is some 1,300 yards, and that between the Māshlun shoulder of Bar-sar and a corresponding elevation on the slope below Būrimār certainly not less than 500 yards. It follows that since the *ballistai* and *katapeltai* forming the Greek artillery of that period could throw stones and darts a distance of only some 300 yards, and slingers and bowmen their missiles not much farther, it was necessary to advance the position from which their 'fire' was to be discharged. This could be done here with effect only in a horizontal direction, for a descent into the ravine would not have increased the chance of commanding the higher slopes.

The ingenious expedient of constructing a mound to secure this object is thus fully accounted for by the configuration of the Būrimār ravine. Similarly, the use made of timber for its construction, whether in the form of stakes or tree-trunks, fully agrees with the abundance of tree growth that can still be seen on the slopes both above and below the Būrimār plateau. Undoubtedly this abundance of timber available on the spot would supply the handiest material for the purpose. That the mound should have been advanced, as is recorded, a stadion or about 200 yards on the first day is readily understood in view of the comparatively easy nature of the slope near the eastern edge of the Būrimār plateau. But it becomes steadily steeper and steeper as the bottom of the ravine is approached, and in consequence the rate of the daily advance necessarily decreased in proportion to the greater depth to be filled up. This explains why, even when on the fourth day a few Macedonians had forced their way to a small hillock on the opposite slope, it was necessary, as Arrian tells us, to continue work on the mound in order to join the two.

I believe that we may safely identify this 'small hillock' with the shoulder of Māshlun, described above. Its level as measured by aneroid is about 450 feet above that of the bottom of the Būrimār-kandao, and about the same above the flat portion of Pīr-sar. It is true that Arrian calls this small hill 'level with the Rock'. But this is easily understood, considering that a continuous slope passing Bar-sar connects Māshlun with the plateau portion of Pīr-sar. That there still rose a steep height above the 'small hillock' is made perfectly clear by Arrian's own narrative, where he describes the stiff climb which brought Alexander and his seven hundred to the top of the 'Rock' after the mound had been joined to the hillock and while the defenders were abandoning Aornos.

I myself retain a very vivid recollection of the trying scramble over steep crags by which I gained the summit of Bar-sar after visiting Māshlun. I can hence realize what this ascent of about 350 feet must have meant for men encumbered by armour. That the height of Bar-sar was a very convenient place for the Macedonians to assemble, and then at a preconcerted signal to turn upon the retreating barbarians, as related by Arrian, is obvious. It is also easy to understand that some of the latter in their panic-stricken flight during the night lost their lives by falling down precipices below Pīr-sar.

CHAPTER XXI

ANCIENT REMAINS AT PĪR-SAR AND THE NAME OF MOUNT ŪṆA

We have now seen how closely all the topographical details of Pīr-sar agree with what our extant records tell us of Aornos and Alexander's operations against it. But antiquarian and philological evidence may be adduced in further support of this identification. There is no suggestion whatsoever in our texts that the natural defences of Aornos had been strengthened by the hand of man, and we may attach all the more significance to this negative fact in view of the obvious desire of our authors to emphasize the greatness of the difficulties overcome before the stronghold was captured. That Aornos was recognized by them to have been a purely natural stronghold is clearly shown by the fact that they ordinarily designate it simply by the term *petra*, 'the Rock'. But we are told by Arrian that Alexander after the capture built there a fortified post and entrusted the charge of it to Sisikottos, an Indian deserter, who had joined him in Baktra and proved trustworthy. Curtius, too, mentions Sisicostus as having been charged with the defence of the 'Rock' and adjoining territory. Curtius further mentions that Alexander erected altars on the 'Rock' to Minerva and Victory, while Arrian refers merely to sacrifices performed there by him.

In view of Arrian's statement, it is of distinct interest that I found the ruinous remains of what undoubtedly was a small fort on the summit of Bar-sar (Fig. 86). The walls occupy all the level space there is on the top, and to the north, towards Lānde-sar, descend also on the slope. They form an irregular quadrilateral, of which the longest side eastwards measures 136 feet and the shortest to the north sixty feet. The walls, five feet thick throughout, are deeply buried in debris and earth, largely humus deposited by decay of the luxuriant forest vegetation that has grown up and flourished, evidently for centuries, among and over the ruins. It was only by a careful search that I was able to trace the lines of the enclosing walls and some small rooms in the southern part of the enclosed area. Such excavation as was possible in the time and with the labour available showed masonry of a type not unlike that found at Bīr-kōṭ and at ancient dwellings of early Buddhist times in Swāt, stone slabs, unhewn but fairly uniform in thickness, being set in mud plaster. Among the potsherds discovered on the floor of one of the rooms there were some showing ornamentation similar to that found at Buddhist sites of Swāt but less finished.

What pointed to considerable antiquity was the far-advanced decay of the whole structure, as compared with the fair condition in which most of the ruined dwellings and fortified mansions dating from Buddhist times are found at Swāt sites. Yet these, by their position, are far more exposed to erosion and other destructive factors than the very top of Bar-sar could be. The position is such as could not have been chosen for any other purpose than defence. Whether the remains in question can go back as far as the Macedonian invasion, and whether they mark the spot where the fort erected under Alexander's orders may have stood, are questions that it is impossible to answer without thorough investigation, such as was not possible at the time of my visit. But it is certainly noteworthy that the ruined fort crowns just that height which protects the Pīr-sar plateau on the side where, as we have seen, it was most exposed to attack.

The old Gujars, who had been summoned from the hamlets below as depositories of local lore (Fig. 88), knew of no special tradition attaching to these ruined walls. Among

85. FIELDS NEAR MIDDLE OF PĪR-SAR RIDGE, WITH BAR-SAR AND LĀNDE-SAR IN DISTANCE.

86. REMAINS OF WALLS OF RUINED FORT ON TOP OF BAR-SAR.

them was Ibrāhīm Bābā, a venerable old man, who was brought up with much trouble in a litter, and was declared to be a fountain-head of local information. He remembered having fought, as a young man between twenty and thirty years of age, against the British at the Ambēla Pass in 1862. Nor had they ever heard of Alexander having visited these parts. But they had been told by their elders that Pīr-sar had served as the summer residence of a Rāja called Sirkap, who otherwise lived below at the village of Sarkul on the Indus opposite Thākōt. This name of 'Rāja Sirkap' is widely attached to ancient sites in these parts on either side of the Indus, e.g. to the ruins of the earliest city at Taxila that has so far been explored. But it gives no clue beyond indicating a traditional belief that the Pīr-sar plateau was occupied in early times long before the advent of Islām. The same Gujar informants derived the name Pīr-sar from a saint called Pīr Bēghan, who is said to have lived on the plateau before the Pathāns took the land, and to have been buried as a saint at the Ziārat, near the centre of Pīr-sar.

Whether any datable remains are concealed in parts of Pīr-sar now under cultivation or occupied by Gujar huts and graveyards, it is impossible to say. But in the mosque that lies some 300 yards south of the Ziārat there are two large carved slabs of white calcareous stone, now used to support the roof, but undoubtedly ancient. Their exposed portions measure some six feet in height. They were said to have been dug up some time ago somewhere near the centre of the area. But nobody could or would indicate the exact spot; my inquiry here, as elsewhere, suggested, no doubt, an intention to hunt for buried 'treasure'.

There still remains the philological evidence to be set forth. It is furnished by the name *Ūṇa*, in Pashtu also spelt *Ūṇṛa*, applied to the peak rising immediately above

Pīr-sar and also to the whole massif. We do not know the exact indigenous form of the local name which the Greek Ἄορνος was intended to reproduce. But if we assume it to have sounded **Avarna*, it is as easy to account for its phonetic transition into modern *Ūṇa* (*Ūṇṛa*) as it is to prove that Ἄορνος was the most likely Greek rendering of it. That the name rendered by Ἄορνος also appealed to Greek ears by its apparent Greek meaning '[the mountain] where there are no birds', is likely enough. We know from the reproductions of other Indian local names how ready Alexander and his companions were to seek an echo of Greek words in the Indian appellations that they heard. But there is not the least reason to doubt that Aornos was meant to render a genuine local name and was not a freely invented Greek designation. That the name *Ūṇa* has a wider local application can safely be inferred from the fact that the appellation *Ūṇa-sar*, 'head of Ūṇa', and not merely *Ūṇa*, is used for the highest portion of the massif.

There is definite philological evidence to show that in the modern name *Ūṇa* (*Ūṇṛa*) pronounced with that peculiar cerebral *ṇ* sound which in Pashtu spelling also figures as *ṇṛ*, we may safely recognize a direct phonetic derivative of an earlier form **Avarna*, the assumed original of Aornos. I have shown elsewhere that the changes involved are such as unquestionably occur in the phonetic development of both Indo-Aryan and Dardic languages.

I have left to the last the discussion of a classical notice which, if it is taken to refer to Aornos, as I believe it must be, is of quasi-chronological interest and indirectly helps to support the proposed location of that stronghold. Chares of Mytilene, one of Alexander's chief officials, is quoted by Athenaeus as having recorded in his history of Alexander a method of conserving snow used at the siege of the Indian 'town of Petra'. According to Chares, we are told, 'Alexander ordered thirty trenches to be dug close to each other and to be filled with snow, branches of trees being also thrown in, in order that the snow in this way may be preserved longer'. I believe that in this stray notice we have a useful indication both of the elevation of the 'Rock' and of the season when Alexander besieged it.

We know from a record of Aristobulos, who shared Alexander's campaign and is quoted by Strabo, that the army, having set out for India from the Paropamisadai, *i.e.* the valleys between the Hindukush and Kābul, after the fall of the Pleiades, spent the winter in the hill territories of the Aspasioi and Assakēnoi, but in the early spring descended to the plains and moved to Taxila, and thence to the Hydaspes and the country of Poros. That the siege of Aornos was the last of the major operations carried out before the crossing of the Indus and the advance to Taxila is quite certain from the concordant records of Arrian and the other historians. It is also certain that this operation was undertaken after Alexander had descended to the plain of the Peshawar valley. We can therefore place that siege neither much before nor much after the month of April 326 B.C.

Now, from my personal experience on this journey and from the climatic conditions previously observed in similar localities on the North-West Frontier, I may safely assert that in April snow could not be found there much below an elevation of 6,000 feet. On the other hand should water be needed for large numbers, the need of preserving snow for drinking purposes on heights situated between 6,000 and 9,000 feet might well arise at a season when the slopes are exposed to the powerful sun of an Indian spring. From what I saw on my way past the Ūṇa peak and the adjacent heights, I believe that the expedient recorded by Chares would probably nowadays also recommend itself if troops were obliged for a time to occupy that high ground and its southern slopes. The spring of the year referred to in this narrative had been quite exceptionally belated. Yet at the time of my visit at the very end of April we found snow only in small sheltered hollows on the northern slopes of Mount Ūṇa and none at all on the south. The fine spring above 'Little Ūṇa' and another at Adramār, about the same distance on the opposite side of the peak, would scarcely suffice for a large force encamped on this part of the range. It would therefore be no more than an act of prudence if a commander, faced by uncertainty as to the length of his stay on those heights, took steps to conserve whatever remained of the winter's snowfall. We thus see that this fragmentary reference also perfectly accords with that combined evidence of texts, topography, and name which has led us to locate Aornos on the rock-girt site adjoining Mount Ūṇa.

CHAPTER XXII

FAREWELL TO AN HISTORIC SITE AND ITS STORY

With so much to examine on the ground and so much to reconstruct of a great episode in the distant past, I had more than enough to occupy my eyes and thoughts during those strenuous but happy days on the heights of Pīr-sar. The longer I studied the ground, with all its formidable obstacles to the movement and even to the mere maintenance of large numbers of men, the more amazed I felt at the unmeasured energy and ambition which led Alexander to attempt the conquest of so inaccessible a mountain fastness. No less surprising appeared the devotion and unremitting endurance of his Macedonians. The mere thought of the vast distances that they had covered since they set out to follow their young king from the shores of the Aegean would have sufficed to cast glamour over the actual scene of one of their many achievements.

The record of this particularly famous exploit, as it has come down to us, might well have seemed, before the scene of it was known, to bear an air rather of romance than of history. Yet now face to face with the tremendous difficulties that nature itself had here opposed to the invaders, I could only wonder that the story of Aornos should have escaped being treated altogether as a mythos. But then the whole tale of Alexander's triumphant achievements from the Mediterranean far into Central Asia and India is full of incidents testifying to such combined energy, skill, and boldness as would be sought rather in a divine hero of legend than in a mortal leader of men.

During the three days of my stay, there was plenty of life on the Pīr-sar plateau. Khāns from the large villages below on the Indus came to visit us, each a petty feudal baron attended by his armed retainers, while strings of

Gujars toiled up with supplies. The Bādshāh's relations with Barādar Khān of Thākōt, the influential chief of the clans across the river, were still strained, and there was good reason to fear that the latter might tamper with the allegiance, only recently secured, of the tribes on the right bank. So a number of forts had been lately built along the river to ward off inroads from that side, and the commanders of these, too, did not fail to put in their appearance. The Sipāh-sālār and all his host bore bravely with exposure and cold. But there was no attempt to disguise their relief when the completion of my task made it possible to fix the date for our departure.

Had I not been obliged to consider the discomforts to which the men were subjected, I should gladly have remained longer on this classical counterpart of 'my' Kashmīr alp, so glorious were the views it offered. To the north rose in a long line the great snowy peaks above Kāna and Tōrwāl (Fig. 80), with their continuation towards parts of the Indus Kohistān that are as yet unexplored. Far away in the distance Shāh 'Ālam's keen eyes recognized the big spur over which a pass leads from Tangīr to his home of exile in Kandia. It cannot be far from the big bend of the Indus where it turns in a narrow cañon to the south, and in 1913 when I crossed from Darēl to Tangīr my eyes must already have rested on this spur.

To the north-east of the Indus my view extended to another personal link with the past; for in the chain of snow-covered mountains that divide the Indus Kohistān from Kāghān there was more than one peak that I must have sighted on evening climbs above my Battakundī camp of the summers of 1904 and 1905. Farther down I could see winding stretches of the greenish waters of the Indus, over 5,000 feet below Pīr-sar (Fig. 87). Beyond to the east the eye wandered over the open valleys of Nandihār

87. INDUS RIVER WITH SNOW-COVERED RANGE TOWARDS KĀGHĀN, SEEN FROM BELOW KUZ-SAR.

88. IBRĀHĪM BĀBĀ AND MĪR WĀLĪ, OF RANZERO HAMLET, WITH OTHER GUJARS EXAMINED ON PĪR-SAR.

and Pakhlī far away to the Murree hills, still glittering here and there with the snow of this abnormally late spring. The distances were far too great to recognize there any of the small hill stations where British troops had already taken up their summer quarters to escape the heat of the plains. But the big massif of the Black Mountains hiding Agrōr and Hazāra seemed quite a close neighbour across the Indus valley. And as the eye followed the river's tortuous course to the south I could clearly see through my glasses how useless it would be to look for another plateau like Pīr-sar among the jumble of chopped and serrated hills stretching down through Pūran and the Chagarzai country towards Bunēr and Mahāban.

It was in that direction that my next moves were to take me. On general grounds it is probable that some of these hill tracts between Bunēr and the Indus had also been visited by Macedonian forces after Aornos had been captured. But the notices left to us of Alexander's movements immediately after that great feat are too brief and divergent in their details to permit us to trace his route with any certainty on the ground. So I may conveniently sum up here what little we are told of the remainder of Alexander's campaign before he crossed the Indus to start on the invasion of the Panjāb.

Arrian (*Anabasis*, IV. XXX. 5) tells us that Alexander moved from the 'Rock' into the territory of the Assakēnoi, having been informed that the brother of Assakēnos, with elephants and a host of neighbouring barbarians, had taken refuge in the mountains of that region. When he reached the town of Dyrta in this territory, he found it, together with the surrounding district, abandoned by its inhabitants. Thereupon he detached certain commanders to examine the localities and to secure information from any barbarians captured, particularly about the elephants. We have seen above that Assakēnos was the ruler whose capital Massaga was taken on the Macedonians' first entry into Lower Swāt. Hence the mountain region in which his brother had taken refuge, and which was reckoned as part of the territory of the Assakēnoi, might well have been Bunēr; for this, as the records of the Chinese pilgrims clearly show, was in ancient times included in Swāt territory, just as it is now once more. But the position of Dyrta has not been identified, and no other indications are furnished.

To Bunēr, however, seems to point what we are next told about Alexander's march on the Indus: 'and the army going on before made a road for him, as those parts would otherwise have been impassable.' This description would well apply, as first suggested by General Abbott, to the most direct route leading from the central parts of Bunēr to the Indus along the Barandu river; for the lower valley of the latter, as yet unsurveyed and in part inaccessible owing to the colony of 'Hindustānī fanatics' at present settled there, is reported to be a narrow gorge in places impracticable for traffic.

From captives Alexander learned that the Indians of that territory had fled to Abisares, *i.e.* to the ruler of Hazāra. They had left the elephants behind by the river, and these Alexander succeeded in capturing. Finally we are told that, serviceable timber having been found by the river, this was cut by the troops and the ships built with it taken down the Indus to where a bridge had long before been constructed by the other portion of the army.

Diodorus' account of what followed the capture of Aornos is very brief. We are told by him that Aphrikes, an Indian chief, was hovering in that neighbourhood with twenty thousand soldiers and fifteen elephants. The chief was killed by his own men, who brought his head to Alexander and thereby purchased their own safety. The elephants wandering about the country were secured by the king, who then arrived at the Indus, and finding it bridged gave his army a rest of thirty days before crossing to the left bank.

Curtius' account, evidently taken from the same source, supplements the above by some details, which, however, do not furnish any clear topographical guidance. Alexander is said to have marched from the 'Rock' to Ecbolima, which evidently is the same place as Arrian's Embolima. Having learned that a defile on the route was occupied by twenty thousand armed men under Erix, he hurried forward, dislodged the enemy with his archers and slingers, and thus cleared a passage for his heavy-armed troops behind. Erix was killed in flight by his own men and his head brought to Alexander. Thence he arrived after the sixteenth encampment at the Indus, where he found everything prepared by Hephaistion for the crossing.

Here, at the starting-point of his invasion of India proper, we must leave the great conqueror. Alexander's triumphal progress through the wide plains of the Panjāb has, owing to the fascination exercised at all times by the wonders of distant India, attracted the chief interest of his historians, ancient as well as modern. But those who are familiar with the natural difficulties of the territories beyond the present North-West Frontier and with their military history in recent times may well be even more impressed by the greatness of the obstacles overcome by Alexander's genius and the pluck and endurance of his hardy Macedonians in the course of the long campaign that preceded the invasion.

CHAPTER XXIII

THROUGH CHAKĒSAR AND PŪRAN

IT was with regret that I took leave of Aornos on the morning of April 30th. I was therefore glad that the long and rather fatiguing march, which brought us down to Chakēsar in the evening, lay for the most part along the Upal range and allowed me to look back again and again on that historic scene; so conspicuous is the position of Pīr-sar on the flank of dominating Ūṇa-sar.

At Chakēsar, the chief place of the valleys held by the Azī-khēl tribe, I felt brought back to the present and to a recent and somewhat turbulent past. The two days that I halted there were pleasant and interesting enough in their own way. On the hill-sides around many ruinous remains were to be seen of walls marking sites of ancient dwelling-places. They evidently had been quarried for centuries to supply stones for the small town and for the supporting walls of cultivation terraces. During the years before the Bādshāh's rule was established, Chakēsar had seen a good deal of fighting between the chief local families. But now their defensive towers had all been razed to the ground and a strong fort built for the Bādshāh's 'Hākim'.

The exposure and fatigue to which the men had been subjected during those happy days on the height of Aornos and the marches to and from it obliged me to make a two days' halt at Chakēsar. It felt warm enough down there at an elevation of a little less than 4,000 feet, and flies and mosquitoes were celebrating spring revels all round my tent. Nevertheless I welcomed the short halt, for I had much writing work to do. It also enabled me to record a hitherto unknown Kohistānī tongue, spoken only by some sixty to eighty households of the small Dard community of Batēra higher up in the gorges of the Indus. Even polyglot

89. AT THE 'MIDDLE MOSQUE' OF CHAKĒSAR.

Rāja Shāh 'Ālam, who had first told me about it, found this form of Kohistānī speech difficult to interpret.

It happened, fortunately, that, besides some men of Batēra whom *saeva paupertas* due to the extreme scarcity of cultivable land in their own country had driven to seek work with Pathān Maliks near Chakēsar, two intelligent visitors from Batēra had just then been drawn to Chakēsar by the fame of a pious Miān teacher. These all spoke Dubērī as well as Pashtu in addition to their own tongue. So the taking down of linguistic specimens of 'Batōchī' for Sir George Grierson's learned analysis did not prove quite so troublesome a business as I had at first expected.

Chakēsar lies close to the meeting-place of four much-frequented routes from Kāna, upper Ghōrband, Pūran, and the Indus valley. There is plenty of good cultivable ground held by the virile Azī-khēl clan in the neighbourhood and in the valleys through which those routes lead. These facts account for the importance of Chakēsar not merely as a local trade centre but also as a seat of Muhammadan theological learning. The visits I paid one evening and again on the morning of my departure to the four 'Schools' of Jumāts, established in the shady courts of different Mosques (Fig. 44), was quite an interesting experience. Half a dozen 'big Mullahs', headed until a year or two ago by Khān-khēlo 'Abdul Jalīl, a famous expounder of the Law belonging to one of the chief Azī-khēl families, are drawing students from all parts of the Frontier region, and also from beyond it, to this quaint semblance of a small medieval University. Since 'Abdul Jalīl's death the fame of the Chakēsar schools was said to have become somewhat dimmed. Yet over a hundred and twenty 'Tālib-ilms' were still to be counted, all of them as well as their teachers maintained in food and quarters by the Pathān landowners of the place, with some contribution from the tithe now levied by the Bādshāh.

The amenities of Chakēsar, in the way of good rations, helpful local patrons, and an equable climate, are evidently appreciated by wandering students even from a distance. Quite a number of the 'undergraduates' imbibing here instruction in Muhammadan law and religious tradition, besides Arabic grammar and a modicum of Persian *belles lettres*, were said to have their homes in different parts of Afghānistān. When I inquired after students with whom I might hold converse in familiar Turkī speech, a jolly-looking greybeard was produced with evident pride, a product of far-famed Bukhāra. He was at first much embarrassed when I addressed him in Turkī; for he had left Central-Asian parts some eleven years before, and even there had been accustomed to use mainly Persian, the speech of learned men. But gradually Turkī came back to his tongue. For fully twenty-seven years he had led the life of a wandering student and, perhaps with good reason, thought himself still far from that standard of knowledge which would allow him to settle down as a guide to others in matters of the holy law.

Another aspect of the Tālib-ilms' life was presented by a ruddy-faced Özbeg youth, Maqdūm by name, whose acquaintance I made at the 'Middle Mosque' on the morning of my departure. His home was at Talikhān, in Afghān Turkestān. He had studied at Kābul and Jalālābād, and now for a year past had found instruction and sustenance to his taste at Chakēsar. He was, of course, pleased to hear himself called up in his Turkī tongue, as he sat in a group with other students under the big Chinārs that shade the paved court in front of the praying-hall, with its well-carved wooden arcade (Fig. 89). But for some little time neither in Turkī nor in any other tongue

90. FOOT OF RUINED STŪPA IN TŌP-DARA, GŌKAND.

91. ʿABDUL JALĪL KHĀN (†), OF CHAKĒSAR, AND FIRŌZ KHĀN, OF UPAL.

would speech come from his lips, though they kept steadily moving.

At last the laughter of those in the crowd watching the one-sided dialogue brought the explanation. The young fellow's throat and mouth were choked with the rice he had hastily crammed in before rising from the big platter containing the morning meal that he shared with five other students. Eating meant for all of them competition in quickness of absorption. As Maqdūm was aware of the keen appetites of the rest, he had taken special care to store away what he considered his due share, before abandoning the treat to them. When he had at last struggled through these embarrassing additional mouthfuls, we had quite a cheery talk together about his past studies and his hope of soon continuing them at Delhi. The modest viaticum I offered him was evidently accepted as ample compensation for the portion of the meal he might have missed.

But not all the frequenters of the Chakēsar seat of learning could be trusted to take so kindly to infidel strangers as did this genial Turkī, coming from what by contrast with India seemed to me like a bit of Eastern Europe. Tālib-ilms are not without reason considered among the more fanatical elements on the Frontier. I could therefore guess the reason why 'Abdul Jalīl Khān, one of the local head-men, a fine upstanding person (Fig. 91), when guiding me through the narrow lanes of Chakēsar, carefully took out his Mauser pistol from its case and in a nonchalant yet significant fashion carried it on his right arm. With polite if needless consideration for what might be my supposed feelings, he declared that it was a precaution he thought advisable on his own account, in view of some unsettled blood-feud. Fortunately there was no occasion for him to show what the automatic discharge of the bullets at close quarters might mean. [Since these lines were written news has reached me that my jovial guide has fallen a victim to vendetta.]

Our march on May 2nd led us across the Kāghlun pass westwards into the wide and fertile valley of Pūran. The picturesque side Nullah through which the ascent lay was clothed with luxuriant vegetation, nourished by a lively little stream cascading amidst moss and fern-covered rocks. With big clematis in full bloom and abundance of flowering creepers amidst evergreen shrubs, the scene seemed as if translated from some favoured Mediterranean region. The top of the ridge which the pass crosses, at about 6,200 feet above sea-level, offered a striking view towards both the head of the Ghōrband valley and the high serrated watershed range, crowned by the bold peaks of Dwasare and Ilam, which divided us from Swāt. Rhododendron-trees in full bloom furnished the escort with glowing crimson nosegays, which they stuck into the muzzles of their rifles. But clouds soon began to shroud the heads of the peaks, and the descent to Alōch, the chief place of Pūran, with its newly built fort, was made under a steady drizzle. The tents came in late and were pitched in pouring rain. But the long wait under otherwise depressing conditions was brightened by the opportune arrival of a heavy mail-bag full of cheering letters. No fewer than three of them came from dear friends dwelling on the flower-decked heights above spring-time Florence.

Two pleasant marches took us thence through fertile Pūran and the adjoining Mukhozai hill tract. These likewise had plenty of fine scenery to offer, never yet seen by European eyes. At Chaugā village (Fig. 92), near where the streams descend from the eastern slopes of rugged Mount Dwasare into Pūran, we halted for a night. It was here that the Bādshāh's invading force, commanded by Aḥmad 'Alī, his Sipāh-sālār and now my protector, had

92. CHAUGĀ VILLAGE IN PŪRAN.

four years before been hemmed in and held fast, for seven long days of intermittent fighting, by the confederated clans of Pūran, Chakēsar, Ghōrband, and Kāna. With justifiable pride the alert Commander-in-chief pointed out to me the steep rocky spurs on either side of the valley from which he at last succeeded in driving the greatly superior force of the besiegers.

Their hold had slackened, probably owing to the failure of supplies from their homes, the usual source of weakness of Pathān tribal gatherings of this kind. Mutual distrust and a want of capacity for common organization, characteristic of such democratic communities on the Frontier, would never allow the clansmen to make systematic arrangements of their own for 'supply and transport'. The importance of these had been duly recognized by the Bādshāh, and the mule corps that he maintains, together with the bridle-roads that he has built to these valleys as well as into other parts of his dominion, must go a long way towards ensuring control over any tribal risings. In Chaugā there were still numbers of houses standing roofless or with badly battered walls. But I noticed no sign of lingering resentment among the local Bābuzai clansmen; like the rest of the Bādshāh's new subjects, they seemed to have accepted with relief the internal peace imposed by his regime—at any rate as a temporary change.

CHAPTER XXIV

TO BUNĒR AND MOUNT ILAM

On May 5th we ascended by a good riding-road the beautiful and fertile main valley of Mukhozai westwards. The well-cultivated fields where the wheat was already ripening betokened the advantages derived here from the absence of the *wēsh* system, which is unknown to the local clan. Lively streams descend from the heights of Dwasare, well over 10,000 feet above the sea, and the fine flowering shrubs on the lower slopes, with much forest higher up, seemed to indicate an adequate rainfall. Large shady plane-trees on green meadowland by the streams recalled Kashmīr.

Then, on the Nawē-ghākhē pass, close on 7,000 feet in height, we reached the north-eastern border of the big territory of Bunēr. From that high ridge an impressively wide view opened over the greater portion of Bunēr (Fig. 93); the bold detached hills that encircle and divide its large valleys rose before me as if on a relief map. With pleasure I greeted again the well-remembered passes and valleys through which I had moved more than twenty-eight years before in the course of my 'archaeological tour with the Bunēr Field Force'. Far away to the east I could take a last farewell view of the far-stretching range that divides Ghōrband and Chakēsar, with the rugged height of Mount Ūṇa standing on guard over its Indus end. Near below on the Bunēr side the eye ranged over boldly serrated hills, all clothed in vivid metallic green, mostly of cedars and firs (Fig. 94).

In the picturesque valley of Gōkand where my camp stood for two nights, at a height of some 4,200 feet, it felt rather hot and close. But a day's long ride down the valley was rewarded by the discovery of interesting ancient remains, which in 1898 had remained beyond my range. Among

93. VIEW TOWARDS MIDDLE PORTION OF BUNĒR FROM NAWĒ-GHĀKHĒ PASS.

them was a fine Stūpa found in the little side valley of Tōp-dara below the village of Bagra (Fig. 90). It proved remarkably well preserved under the luxuriant growth of vegetation, including wild fig and other trees, which had managed to effect a lodgement in the solid masonry of the hemispherical dome and its triple base. A fine spring issuing near the ruins no doubt accounted for the choice of the site, and in the heat of the day was doubly grateful to men and ponies. The season from here onwards began unpleasantly to remind me of the advance that the 'hot weather' had already made in the plains.

On the 7th May I made my way across the Rājgalai pass to Pācha, a large village containing the most famous shrine of Bunēr, the tomb of the saintly hermit known simply by the name of Pīr Bābā, 'the holy old man'. On the way I stumbled, as it were, upon the ruins of a smaller Stūpa, which, half smothered under the debris and refuse accumulations from adjoining Gujar hovels, had remained apparently unknown to my local informants. At Pācha, which I well remembered from my first visit with the Bunēr Field Force during the punitive expedition of 1898, I halted for two days under the walls of the Bādshāh's moated fort, partly in consequence of the keen desire of all my companions to pay prolonged devotions to the powerful saint and partly owing to heavy rain. Fortunately the latter gave place for a time to mere drizzling vapour and mist, and allowed me to examine some curious ancient towers and habitations at Ramanai, high up on an outlier of Mount Ilam (Fig. 96). But it was a somewhat exhausting experience of an aerial Turkish bath. There was no ignoring the fact that over the big open valleys of Bunēr the hot weather had begun to set in, the elevation of Pācha being only about 2,500 feet.

So I felt quite glad when on May 10th I was able to start

for the last item on my programme of exploration. It was the visit to the summit of Mount Ilam, the most conspicuous landmark of both Swāt proper and Bunēr. Legends of ancient date, as the account of Hsüan-tsang proves, cluster round the peak. It raises its conical head of precipitous crags to 9,200 feet, in noble isolation above the wooded spurs which radiate from it. The ascent, which occupied two days, started just above the large village of Bai. I remembered it well from a bitterly cold night I had spent near it in January 1898, bivouacking with my old friend General L. C. Dunsterville, then a young captain, and his old regiment, the xxth Punjabis.

The first march brought us by the evening to the small village of Ilam-kile, nestling in alpine seclusion between the main peak and the rugged outlier of Alak-sar rising to the south of it. The stiff climb along cliffs and round deep-cut ravines was made pleasant by the varied zones of vegetation that we traversed. Lower down the eye could feast on the wonderful display of velvety orange-red blossoms hanging in clumps from the bare branches of trees in which I recognized with surprise the 'Dāk' of the Western Panjāb plains. Evidently the shelter and warmth afforded by the southern aspect of the slopes had allowed these trees to establish themselves on heights up to about 3,500 feet. Higher up, violets and a great variety of flowers, familiar to me but retaining as it were their incognito, owing to my botanical ignorance, were spread in profusion wherever fertile loam hid the chalk and granite rock. It was pleasant to think that this floral wealth had already attracted the notice of old Hsüan-tsang, fixed as his eyes mainly were on things sacred and spiritual.

This is what his narrative tells us:

Above 400 *li* south from Mêng-chieh-li is the *Hi-lo* mountain. The stream of the mountain valley flows west; as you go up it east-

94. VIEW DOWN GŌKAND VALLEY FROM ABOVE SHŌDARA.

95. CRAGS OF MAIN SUMMIT OF MOUNT ILAM.

ward flowers and fruits of various kinds cover the watercourse and climb the steeps. The peaks and precipices are hard to pass, and the ravines wind and curve. You may hear the sound of loud talking or the echo of musical strains. Square stones like couches made by art form an unbroken series over the gulley. It was here that Buddha once in a former birth gave up his life for the hearing of a half-stanza of doctrine.

The identification of the 'Hi-lo mountain' with Mount Ilam, long ago conjectured by M. Foucher, was proved to be right by the evidence relating to those 'square stones like couches' furnished by my visit to the summit. And though the distance indicated from Mêng-chieh-li or Manglawar (corresponding roughly to eighty miles or so) is certainly wrong, our Chinese pilgrim guide was right in describing the stream of the mountain valley as flowing west. The principal drainage from the massif is down the valley that descends to below the Bunēr side of the Karākar pass, *i.e.* to the west-south-west, and it is by this that the easiest route, usually followed by modern Hindu pilgrims, leads up to the Jōgiān-sar end of the summit. So once again my patron saint's sense of topography has been vindicated, at least as regards the bearing.

At more than one point of the ascent we had passed ruins of ancient dwellings and traces of terraced fields abandoned ages ago. But what I enjoyed more was the delightful coolness of our camp that night in the well-screened little basin where the fields and farms of Ilam village nestle at an elevation of close on 6,000 feet. That they belong to Miāns, supposed descendants of the holy 'Pīr Bābā' of Pācha, seemed curiously to accord with the sacred character that had attached to the mountain in Buddhist times.

From Ilam-kile the final climb of some 3,000 feet to the top of the peak was accomplished before midday of May 11th. It led first over well-wooded slopes to a dip in the watershed towards the Jaosu pass, where I came in sight of the Swāt river and the lower ends of the valleys that I had visited round Mingaora and Saidu. Then the climb took us steeply over and between big masses of much-weathered rock, often undercut and carved into quite fantastic shapes by prolonged water action. In places precipitous gullies, still deeply filled with snow, were crossed amidst a thick growth of firs and pines.

Then at last we reached the tower-like mass of rock forming the main summit. It is crowned by four isolated crags like the pinnacles of a square church tower, and is difficult of access. The easternmost of these forms on its top a small platform, artificially enlarged with trunks of trees (Fig. 95). Ancient local worship, continued in its present Hindu guise, has located here the throne of Rāmachandra, an incarnation of Vishnu. Hither an annual pilgrimage brings many Hindu shopkeepers with their families from the villages of Lower Swāt, as well as from adjacent parts of the border. Gujars, too, in pious rivalry claim the spot as the resting-place, of course, of a martyr or 'Shahīd' of the true Faith.

The distant panoramic view enjoyed from these crags was truly magnificent. From the great snowy ranges of the Swāt Kohistān and of the Hindukush beyond Dīr and the bend of the Indus it extended over the whole of Upper Swāt and Bunēr right down to the plain of Yusufzai. A hot-weather haze lay over the more distant parts of the plain and hid Peshawar with the mountains of Tirāh and the Safēd-koh above Kābul. But these, too, are within view after rain or in the clear atmosphere of the autumn. It was an ideal spot from which to bid farewell to the varied tracts from which it had been my good fortune 'to lift the Purdah'.

But Mount Ilam rarely fails to wear a cap of cloud after midday; so I had soon reason to leave its age-worn head.

96. VIEW ACROSS BUNĒR FROM RAMANAI SPUR.
Remains of ancient habitations in foreground.

97. HOLLOW ON TOP OF MOUNT ILAM, WITH SACRED SPRING AND HSÜAN-TSANG'S 'STONE COUCHES'.

Descending over the precipitous crags for some two hundred feet I found the small tree-girt hollow which holds the little spring and a string of round limpid pools fed by it. They are worshipped by Hindu pilgrims as sacred features of the site. My eyes rested with particular pleasure on the large flat-topped rocks stretching along the pools (Fig. 97); for there could be no doubt that Hsüan-tsang had them in mind when he referred to the 'square stones like couches', shaped as if by the hand of man, which were to be seen on Mount 'Hi-lo'.

The little hollow or saddle between the two summits is only some hundred and fifty yards across. So our camp, with the tents of the Sipāh-sālār, his men, &c., was closely packed in its romantic setting. The two nights we spent there were decidedly cold, with hoar-frost still on the ground when the sun rose. But there were big logs burning to warm the men, and the Sipāh-sālār's jovial old chef had quite a cosy kitchen under a large rock fantastically hollowed out like the upper jaw of a fossilized Saurian.

CHAPTER XXV

DEPARTURE FROM SWĀT

THE morning of the 13th May saw us set out for the valley which leads to Saidu. The very steep descent along a rugged buttress of the mountain led us to the little alp of Sarbāb on its northern side, where the Bādshāh has established his summer quarters, and farther on to the fort and hamlet of Miāna, where we camped. On the following day we moved down the valley past Kukrai and Batēra, which we had already visited in March from Saidu, and regained the Swāt capital. There a most hearty welcome awaited me from its ruler.

A suite of little rooms, rather stuffy and dark, quite close to the Bādshāh's airy reception hall, was set apart for me. A walled-in little court in front suggested that they had once served for the accommodation of the ladies of the chief's family. There I spent a day busily occupied in receiving farewell visits from those who had shared my travels and in distributing suitable presents. The Chief Commissioner had been kind enough to provide them for me out of his own 'Tōshakhāna' in special recognition, as he put it, of the 'political' value of my tour. Both in my own temporary quarters and in the private apartment of the Bādshāh I had long talks with the ruler who, like an old friend, discoursed freely on the trials and struggles of the past and his plans for the future.

On the morning of May 16th I said my heartfelt parting thanks to my kind host and protector, the Bādshāh, his promising heir-apparent Shāhzāda Jahānzeb Sāhib, and the chief supporters of his rule. In the course of less than four hours the Bādshāh's motor-lorry carried me, along with Sipāh-sālār and Rāja Shāh 'Ālam, on the unmetalled road that had been open for a year to the Malakand. The country traversed had become familiar to me during March; but now there was an opportunity of collecting my varied impressions into one picture of rural wealth in the big main valley of 'Udyāna'. Far sooner than I wished the *enceinte* and grim medieval-looking towers of the Malakand were reached, and under the hospitable roof of Mr. Metcalfe, the Political Agent, perched high above the pass, my Swāt expedition came to its end.

Gladly would I have extended it yet for months, but for the call of a heavy piece of literary work awaiting completion, and also a sense of the trouble to which my kind host and his people had already been put by my tour. A hurried visit to Peshawar, now sweltering in its hot-weather atmosphere, was followed by a short but most enjoyable stay on the cool wooded heights of Nathiagali, the summer head-quarters of the North-West Frontier Province. There Colonel Keen's kind hospitality enabled me to see that ever-helpful friend once more, and to supplement my previous reports by word-of-mouth descriptions of what I had seen of the land, its capable master, and its people. Then a brief halt at Murree allowed me to acquaint Captain W. J. Norman, Deputy Director of the Frontier Circle of the Survey of India, with the mapping results achieved through Surveyor Tōrabāz Khān's devoted exertions, before I regained Kashmīr. But even from the glorious height of my beloved alpine camp, my thoughts have since constantly reverted with delight to the happiest wandering that I ever enjoyed between the Pāmīrs and the Indian Ocean.

FINIS

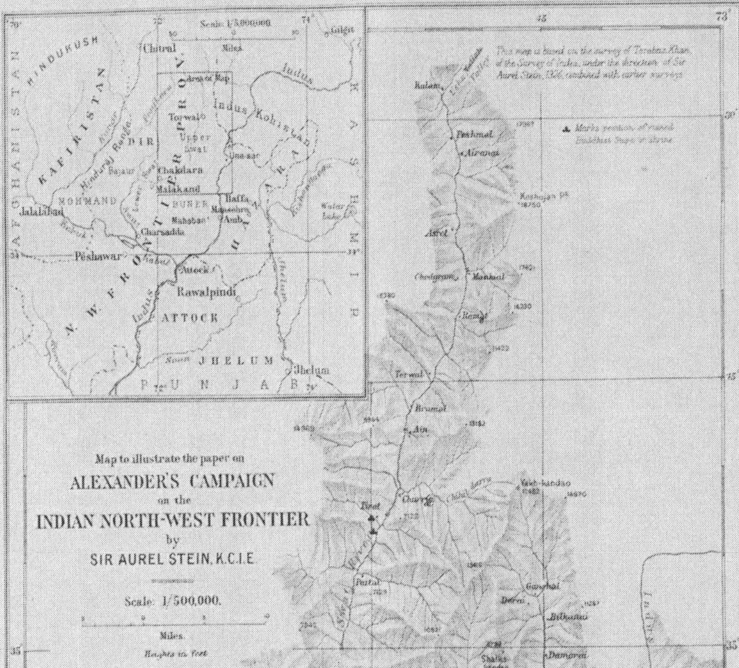

Published by permission of the Royal Geographical Society

ALEXANDER'S CAMPAIGN
INDIAN NORTH-WEST FRONTIER
Stein

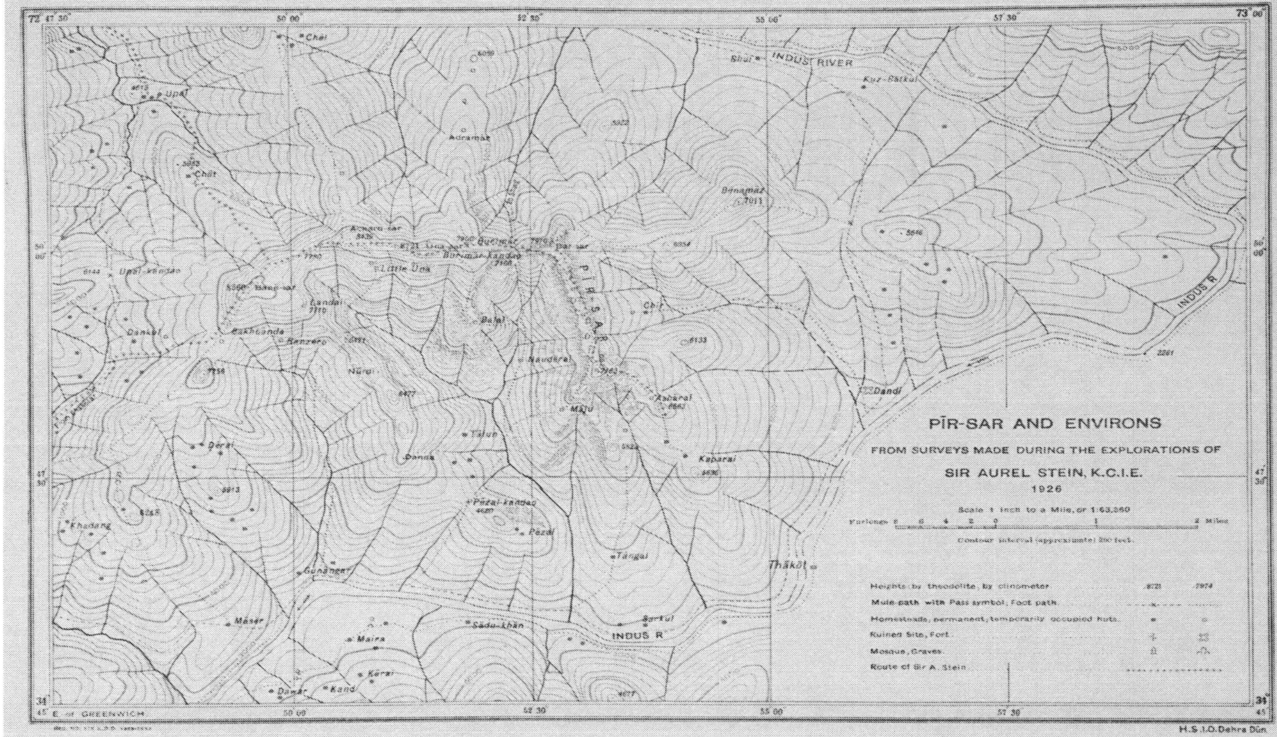

PĪR-SAR AND ENVIRONS
FROM SURVEYS MADE DURING THE EXPLORATIONS OF
SIR AUREL STEIN, K.C.I.E.
1926
Heights by theodolite, by clinometer
Mule-path with Pass symbol; Foot path
Homesteads, permanent, temporarily occupied huts.
Ruined Site, Fort.
Mosque, Graves.
Route of Sir A. Stein
INDUS RIVER
INDUS R
Kuz-Ratkul
Dandi
Thākōt
Kaparai
Tangai
Sarkul
Sādu-khān
Maira
Kerai
Kand
Māser
Gunangar
Pazal
Talun
Danda
Māju
Nauderai
Bajal
Nūrai
Ranzero
Bakhtanda
Landai
Little Ūna
Burimar-kandao
Adramar
Benamaz
Chir
Chēl
Upal
Chūt
Upal-kandao
Dankal
Dērai
Khadang
Dawār
E. of GREENWICH
H.S. I.O. Dehra Dūn

INDEX